Embracing
the
Extraordinary

PETER, KARYN,

MAY THE LOVE OF CHRIST
CONTINUE TO FILL YOUR LIFE
AND MAY HE CONTINUE TO BE
YOUR SOLACE IN ALL THAT YOU DO.

IN HIS LOVE,

Kevin Graham

Joyce Graham

EPH 3:14-21
COL 1:15-23

Embracing the Extraordinary

Steven Foster Graham

MILESTONES
INTERNATIONAL PUBLISHERS

Embracing the Extraordinary: A Story of God's Eternal Faithfulness

ISBN: 978-1-935870-03-6
UPC: 88571300073-4

Printed in the United States of America.

© 2011 by Steven F. Graham

MileStones International Publishers
PO Box 104, Newburg, PA 17240

303.503.7257; Fax: 717.477.2261

www.milestonesintl.com

1 2 3 4 5 6 7 8 / 15 14 13 12

Dedication

As you read this book you will readily see that my lovely wife Joyce is an integral part of everything that I have shared with you. By God's grace she has been my companion, my help, and my balancing influence as we have made this journey from young, naive, clueless teenagers to those who love God beyond life. Through good and bad she has always been there with me as we have traveled this uncertain, uneven, uncompromising path learning together to know Christ more. Without her there would be no story.

What more can I say except to paraphrase Proverbs 31, and declare: I have found a wife of noble character, a wife who fears the Lord. She is worth far more than rubies. My heart has confidence in her as she has brought me and our children good all the days of her life. She watches over her household and has never been idle but has continually given herself to us. We give her praise and say, "Many women have been wonderful wives and mothers, but in our eyes you surpass them all."

Acknowledgments

Thank you to my wife, Joyce, without whom there would be no story to tell and to whom this book is dedicated.

Thank you to the Timarron Country Club employees and contractor whose immediate response in getting me out of my pickup, administering CPR, and using the defibrillator unit within the first few minutes of my heart stopping, saved my life. Without their actions I would not have survived.

Thank you to my children who came together in a difficult time, pouring out their love and tender care for their mother and me to see us through the crisis.

Thank you to all of our friends and the pastors from Gateway Church who stood by Joyce and my family with their prayers and emotional support and helped her and my family through the crisis of my cardiac arrest.

Thank you to all of those we do not know personally across the U.S. and in foreign countries who prayed for us just because we needed their prayers and were part of His Church.

Thank you to all of those whom God has brought into our life, whom God has used to make our life richer, and who have helped us see more of Christ in our life's journey together.

Thank you to Jim and Tonya Rill for accepting this book project and shepherding it through to its completion.

Table of Contents

An Extraordinary Event

Note to the Reader

The events of Thursday, October 30, 2008, and of the days that followed as described in Part One of this book are based on the accounts given to me by friends and family because I have no conscious memory of the day of my sudden cardiac arrest or of the next nine days.

Chapter One

"It Can't Be My Husband"

When I started the day on Thursday, October 30, 2008, I did not know that it would bring the most traumatic event of my life. It was a crisp, clear day in north central Texas. It was, I had to admit, a great day for playing golf. At first I had been reluctant to accept Joe Christ's invitation to play a round with him and two other men at the Timarron Country Club. Joe was a good friend of mine and a fellow member of the Saturday evening "PrimeTime" (over 50) class at Gateway Church. My reluctance had nothing to do with Joe or the other two men, but with the fact that I no longer played golf. I had given up the game several years earlier, concluding that it took too much time, energy, and money to play at an acceptable level, particularly when there were many other things in my life that were more important to me.

But the more I thought about it, the more I realized that this would be a good way to enjoy some fellowship with a few of the other men in the class. A little wifely persuasion from Joyce also helped me make up my mind. I called Joe and told him I would be glad to join him and the others for the game. Now that the day had come, and with such perfect weather, I actually found myself looking forward to the outing.

At one point as I was getting ready to leave I was standing in the breakfast area of our home, gazing out the back door, lost in my own thoughts. Joyce walked over and put her hand on my arm. "What's on your mind, Steve?" she asked gently. She knew very well that faraway look in my eyes.

I was, in fact, reflecting on many things that morning. For one, I was contemplating our present and our future—where we were and what lay ahead of us. I was getting ready to retire from my job with an international public accounting firm. After working since I was 9 years old, I was, at age 68, finally going to stop working full-time. We had no debt and everything looked bright for our future. I was healthy, ate right, exercised regularly, and was always careful to get an annual physical. In fact, as part of my annual physical for that year, only a few months earlier, I had worn a heart monitor for a month. My doctor concluded that my heart was in perfect condition. I had no known risk factors for heart problems of any kind. Joyce was healthy also, and our adult children and their families were all doing well. The years ahead indeed looked bright.

In response to Joyce's question, I said, "I was just thinking how much I desire to see all of the Church become all that the Lord has called it to be. I long to see all the men and women in Christ's Church understand the fullness of His love and become all that He has called us be; that out of the normal outworking of our relationship with Christ, we will see more people prayed for and healed and even some raised from the dead."

Little did I know that I was about to experience personally part of the very thing I longed to see.

After a pleasant drive in my pickup to the Timarron Country Club, I met up with Joe and the other two men in the parking lot. We unloaded our gear and checked in at the club. When our tee time arrived, we advanced to the first tee and started our game. We had a great time playing golf together and talking about the Lord and various and sundry other subjects. I always enjoy fellowship with people who love the Lord.

On the 18th hole, my approach shot skipped across the top of the water guarding the green and rolled up to a place that left me in a good position for my putt. Joe just shook his head and said, "After a shot like that, we better start calling you 'Skippy' Graham." We all laughed at his joke and finished the hole.

We were still laughing about my "trick" shot and my new nickname as we made our way back to the clubhouse. In the parking lot, we shared some parting words, stowed our golf gear in our respective vehicles, and got ready to drive home. I climbed into my pickup, started the engine, and began making my way up the exit road that curved around in front of the clubhouse. It had been an enjoyable afternoon. As I rounded the curve and approached the clubhouse, my thoughts moved ahead to plans for the evening. I did not know that I was seconds away from an event that would change my life.

I Did Not Know that I Was Seconds Away From an Event that Would Change My Life

Joe was just getting into his vehicle when he heard a loud crunching sound from the direction of the clubhouse. He could not see me, but what he did see was smoke and the back of a truck that belonged to two plumbers, who were working on a project for the Club. Joe's first thought was, "Oh no, Steve has had a wreck!" He ran up the road to see if I was all right but as soon as he saw the situation, he knew that there was a serious problem. My pickup truck had smashed into a stone retaining wall a few feet from the front door of the clubhouse. The engine was still running, the rear tires were spinning so fast they were throwing rubber against the wheel wells, the cab was filling with smoke, and Joe knew immediately that I was in trouble. What he did not realize, however, was that I was already dead.

David Strickland, the lead plumber, had turned in his invoice for the work that had been done and was coming out of the front door just as my truck hit the wall. He was shocked to see that my pickup had just missed the back of his truck where he had been standing just a few minutes before. Seeing that my head was thrown back, my arms were stiff with my hands holding to the steering wheel, I was not moving, and my legs were stretched out with my right foot pressing down on the accelerator, he knew that he had to quickly do something. Realizing that my pickup doors were locked and that no one could get inside to help me, he immediately ran to his truck, got a sledgehammer, ran back to my pickup, and broke out the passenger side window (not an easy thing to do). He then opened the door, got in the truck, and turned the engine off. By this time Joe had arrived at the pickup. Leaning in the passenger side of the cab, he grabbed my ankles to pull me from the truck. At that same moment, Mike Goff, the Club general manager, and a club guest arrived to lift my upper body. Mike saw that I was turning an ashen blue color and quickly checked for my pulse, but he could not find one. Together, the three of them lifted me out of the pickup and laid me down on the road a short distance away. All the while this was going on, Joe was silently crying out to God, "Lord, please don't let Steve die!" Joe had lost two sons and he knew the pain of death. He did not want to experience that pain with a friend.

Joe stood by and continued to pray even as Canaan Pierce from the Pro Shop ran up with the Club's Automated External Defibrillator unit (AED) and handed it to Andy Jacobs, the Club's sous chef who had just arrived. Andy and Mike prepared the unit. Kenny Bredemeire, the assistant golf pro, had arrived ready to start CPR.

Kenny ripped open my shirt and he and the club guest immediately began to perform CPR while Andy and Mike connected the defibrillator unit and followed its procedures. They had gotten the defibrillator unit and received their training just two weeks before and they knew exactly what to do. While these men worked on me, someone else on the scene dialed 911 while Susan Merrill, membership director, took charge and made sure the area was quickly blocked off, that someone was directing traffic, and that the area was ready for the paramedics who were on the way. In the meantime, Kenny provided breath to me and the guest continued giving me chest compressions. While they were using the defibrillator, it kept telling them that they were not pressing hard enough when doing the compressions, so they pressed even harder.

"Clear!"

Everyone around me broke physical contact with me as the defibrillator automatically administered its calibrated electrical charge to my heart through the pads attached to my chest.

Nothing.

"Again!"

A second jolt surged through my heart.

"I've got a pulse!" Kenny called out. "But it's faint."

The AED gave me a third shock. This time my pulse was stronger. I had a clear heartbeat and a little color began to return to my face. By now the ambulance had arrived, and the EMTs took over.

Six minutes had passed since they started trying to save me.

Six minutes plus the time it took to get me out of the truck with no heartbeat, no breath. In most other situations we would not care about a few minutes going by. But when a sudden cardiac arrest happens, when the electricity to the heart turns off, when there is no flow of life-sustaining, oxygen-rich blood to the brain, the first few minutes are critical. Brain damage can start to occur in just a few minutes after the heart has stopped. Based on information from several heart associations, approximately 300,000 to 350,000 incidents of sudden cardiac arrest (SCA) occur in the U.S. each year. Approximately 95% of those who experience SCA die within the first four to six minutes. Only approximately 5% survive and only approximately 1% survive with no heart or brain damage.1 More than enough time had lapsed for me to have resulting severe brain and/or heart damage. What would be the outcome in my case?

In their professional and thoroughly capable manner, the EMTs took over, quickly stabilized me, and transported me to Baylor Hospital in Grapevine. Joe followed them to the hospital. I was alive—barely—but no one knew what the outcome would be.

While I was playing golf at Timarron, Joyce made her weekly visit to the nursing home to check on her aunt and cousin who lived there. She returned home late in the afternoon and had just started preparing supper when the phone rang. At first she ignored it. It was not unusual for us to get advertising calls at that time of day, and she assumed this was another one. After a short interval of time, the phone rang again, and again she ignored it. When it rang the third time, and she realized it was the same number, she began to get suspicious. Something inside told her, "You need to take this call."

Joyce picked up the receiver. "Hello," she said tentatively.

"Are you Mrs. Steven Graham?" a man's voice asked.

"Yes, I am."

"Mrs. Graham, I'm sorry to inform you that your husband, Steve, has had a heart attack and they are taking him to Baylor Hospital in Grapevine."

"Oh no, you must be mistaken," Joyce protested. "My husband is in perfect health. He could not have had a heart attack. There is another Steve Graham who lives in this area; it must be him."

"Was your husband playing golf at Timarron Country Club today?"

"Yes, he was," Joyce replied. A cold knot of fear began to form at the pit of her stomach.

"Then I am afraid we are talking about the same Steve Graham," the man said with compassion in his voice. "Your husband has had a heart attack. They performed CPR on him on-site, and they are taking him to Baylor Grapevine Hospital. You need to get there right away. I would hurry, if I were you."

"Your Husband Has Had a Heart Attack. You Need to Get to the Hospital Right Away."

Joyce hung up the phone in shock. She was so weak, she could barely stand up. Her mind simply couldn't take it in. Steve? A heart attack? How could that be? I was the picture of health! And yet it had happened. I was on my way to the hospital, and the caller told Joyce she needed to get there right away. From her experience as a nurse, Joyce knew that could mean only one thing: my condition was very serious, so serious that I might not make it.

She sank down onto the couch, still holding the phone. "What am I going to do?" She knew she was in no condition to drive. Then she remembered. "Matt is home. I'll call him." Matt is our son. Quickly, Joyce dialed Matt's number, her heart in her throat. Her call went to Matt's voicemail. She dialed a second time. Again voicemail. When her third attempt also went to voicemail, Joyce tossed the phone down on the couch in frustration, threw her hands up, and cried out, "God, please help me!"

The moment after she uttered her cry, the phone rang. It was Matt. She snatched it up quickly. "Oh, Matt! Thank God!"

"Were you trying to call me, Mom?" he asked."

"Yes," Joyce replied, trying to keep her voice calm. "I just got a call from the golf course. Your father has had a heart attack and is on his way to Baylor Grapevine Hospital. They had to perform CPR."

"What?" Matt exclaimed in astonishment. "Dad? He was playing golf? But he doesn't play golf anymore and he can't have had a heart attack"

"I couldn't believe it either," Joyce said, "but it's true. They said it is very serious and that we need to get there as quickly as possible. Can you drive me? I don't think I can drive myself."

"Sure thing, Mom. I'll be right there."

Matt and his family lived just around the block, so he was there at the house in just a couple of minutes. Joyce was already waiting for him. She jumped in the car and they took off for Baylor Grapevine Hospital.

"I can't believe it," Matt said, shaking his head. "When I saw your number on my phone, I didn't think anything of it. The last thing I expected was to hear that Dad had a heart attack and needed CPR. He just had a stress test, and it came back fine. This just doesn't make any sense." As a firefighter and paramedic, Matt was always getting secondhand reports full of misinformation in an emergency situation. He was having a hard time accepting that this had really happened.

Traffic was at a rush hour crawl, which just made their anxiety level that much higher. Matt turned on the car's flashers and started driving on the shoulder of the road. He later said that it felt like he was responding to an emergency call at work, only ten times more intense. Keeping one hand on the wheel, Matt tried several times to call his twin brother, Brad, but kept getting Brad's voicemail.

Since they did not know what they would find when they got to the hospital, Joyce really wanted Brad to be there with them. About halfway to the hospital, when they had not heard from Brad, she called Brad's cell phone number. To her immense relief, he answered with his usual, "This is Brad."

Joyce quickly told Brad what had happened. His initial response was the same as Matt's. "Dad was playing golf?"

"We don't know his condition, other than that it is serious," Joyce told him, "so please hurry."

"I will," Brad promised. "I am conducting a meeting at the moment, which is why I did not answer Matt's calls; I was going to call back after the meeting was over. But when your number came up on the phone, I knew something was wrong. You never call me at work unless it is something very important. Let me close the meeting and I'll be at the hospital as soon as I can."

As Joyce and Matt walked through the door of the hospital emergency room, the first person they saw was Joe Christ. He was noticeably shaken by what had happened. Trying to calm her own nerves and be as upbeat as possible, Joyce managed to smile at Joe and asked, "So how was the golf game?"

Surprised by her question, Joe answered slowly, "It was okay."

Then, in a more subdued tone, Joyce asked, "How's Steve?"

"I don't really know," Joe replied. "They have not told me anything.

As you know, under HIPAA rules they can give specific information only to family members." Joe then told Joyce and Matt in detail what had happened at Timarron.

A few minutes later, a nurse from the ER came out, and after verifying that Joyce and Matt were family members, she advised them that the doctor would be out shortly to talk to them. When Doctor Moustapha appeared, he directed them to a small room where they could talk privately. With their medical training and experience, Joyce and Matt both realized that this was not a good sign. Every ER has a little room with a couch and chairs, where family members await word on the status of a sick or injured loved one. Too often, they had seen confused and frightened family members succumb to grief and tears upon receiving bad news. Is this what awaited them? Joyce and Matt braced themselves to hear the worst.

As the doctor began to talk to them, he spoke in layman's terms, making it apparent that he assumed, quite naturally, that they lacked the perspective of medical training. Joyce quickly interrupted him. "Not to be rude, doctor," she said, "but I am a nurse and my son here is an EMT. All we want to know is if Steve is alive." The doctor relaxed, relieved that he could speak plainly. "Your husband is alive, barely," he said gently. "Good," Joyce said. "We can deal with that."

The doctor was a little taken aback by her answer but then continued, "When he arrived in the ER, your husband's heart was working at about 20% capacity. His condition is grave. We have taken an MRI and my initial examination leads me to believe he has a slight blockage in the left anterior descending artery. We are using hypothermia protocol, which will keep his body at 94 degrees and in a drug-induced coma for three days. We will implant a stent but we will not know the extent of any heart or brain damage he has sustained until we take him off the hypothermia treatment and bring him out of the coma."

The doctor then took Joyce and Matt to the ER room where I was and asked Joyce to verify that I was her husband and then sign all the papers they needed to do the necessary procedures. All Joyce could see outside the hypothermia blanket were my fingers and my nose, but she told the doctor that it was me and then sat down to sign everything that she needed to sign.

Once Joyce and Matt had found out where things were with me and completed the required paperwork, I was taken to the cath lab operating room and they went to the cath lab waiting room. There Matt called his wife Deb to tell her what was going on. He then called his older brother Mike and filled him in. After expressing his initial shock at the news of my heart attack, Mike assured Matt that he and his wife Debbie would leave right away. They lived two hours away. Then Matt called his sister Cindy in Pennsylvania. Cindy was not there, but Matt spoke to her husband, John, who assured Matt that he would pass on the word to Cindy. Matt also found Joe to tell him what the doctors had said and what they were doing.

After I came back from the catheterization to ICU, Joyce and Matt were allowed into my room. It was a scary sight to them to see me covered in the hypothermia blanket, with only the tip of my nose and part of my eyes visible. The whole situation seemed so unreal; they still had trouble accepting that it was really happening.

Thankfully, one of the pastors from Gateway Church had arrived to pray with them and give them support. About 6:30 or 7:00 that evening, Joyce and Matt were directed to the ICU waiting room. They were encouraged to see Joe and Donna Christ waiting for them. Joe and Donna had gotten sandwiches and drinks for everyone. Joyce was unable to eat because of knots in her stomach so large that she could hardly breathe, but she was very thankful for the love and support of these friends who had gathered to wait with her.

By this time Brad had also arrived and Joyce and Matt quickly updated him on the situation.

"From all appearances, there doesn't seem to be a lot of hope," Matt said. "In my 11 years as a firefighter and paramedic, I have been involved in only two CPR cases where we were able to get a pulse and blood pressure back. There are so many variables that have to work perfectly together to make it a successful resuscitation. Judging from what I've heard so far, it's a miracle that Dad is even still alive. And even if he makes it, he faces a long road ahead."

"It's a Miracle that Dad is Even Still Alive."

At the same time that my family and friends were in the ICU waiting room, other families were also there awaiting the outcome of loved ones who had suffered some trauma. During the three days that I was in the hypothermia coma, two of the other ICU patients died. One was an elderly man with a heart problem who was in the room next to mine. The other was a woman with twin teenage daughters, who had suffered a stroke. Witnessing the grief of this family at the loss of this wife and mother in the prime of her life was difficult for Joyce. It made her think even more about my condition and the fact that we have twin sons. This connection made the other family's loss hit especially close to home. Silently, Joyce asked God to comfort them. She realized anew just how fragile life is and how quickly it can change. Even though she knew the outcome with me was in God's hands, she kept thinking what a great blessing it would be to see me come through it all and fully recover.

That Thursday night, as Joyce sat in the ICU waiting room thinking back on all that had happened that day, she suddenly realized that she had not called Wes Pool, the Ernst & Young Tax partner for whom I worked. Joyce knew that Wes was more than just another tax partner and work colleague to me. More than once I had told her how much I enjoyed the times when Wes and I discussed sports, especially "old time" baseball. It never ceased to amaze me that even though Wes was more than 20 years younger than I, he knew more than I did about games and players from the past.

"We need to call Wes," Joyce said, "but I don't have his number."

"I think I can find it," Matt said. "Joe gave me all of Dad's personal effects from the pickup when we got here, including Dad's cell phone. I'm sure Wes's number is in there."

Matt quickly found the number, called Wes, and filled him in on what had happened and what they knew about my condition. Wes arrived at the hospital 20 minutes later and he came by almost every day after that. Wes informed others of my co-workers at Ernst & Young about the situation, and many of them called Joyce to express their support and concern. Some of them even stopped by for a visit. In addition, Wes also made sure that the office sent snacks and drinks for my family and friends in the waiting room. Joyce told me later what a blessing it was to her to see such genuine love and concern coming even from my workplace.

Around 7:30 or 8:00 p.m. the doctor came into the waiting room. Joyce, Matt, Brad, and our gathered friends waited anxiously to hear what he had to say.

"Mrs. Graham," he began, "your husband did have a slight blockage in the left anterior descending artery. We have implanted a stent in that artery. The rest of his heart looks very good and I did not see any other problem with the artery. It will be a little while before you can see him because we have to finish hooking up all of the machines that are keeping him alive. Someone will come get you when we are ready."

The wait seemed longer than it was, but eventually a nurse came out and led my family to my room. When Joyce walked in, one of the first things she noticed was how cold I was. The swish, swish sound of the breathing machine that was keeping me alive seemed ominously loud in the small room. At that moment, Joyce was thankful to be a nurse because, even though it was hard for her to see her husband hooked up to all these machines, it did not shock her. She had seen the same thing before with other patients. Joyce could hardly imagine what it would be like for family members to see all of this surrounding their loved one for the first time.

As soon as Brad entered the room, he went over, sat down beside the bed, held my hand, and prayed for me. Knowing me very well, he prayed simply, "God, please do not take him. I am not ready for that yet. I know that he would rather be with You, but please, do not listen to him this time and answer my prayer to heal him."

Matt was also praying for me. All day, ever since he first heard of my heart attack, Matt had not thought much past the idea of my just staying alive. He struggled to set aside his paramedic experience and be optimistic; in his work he had seen so many heart attack victims die. Sobering questions kept invading his mind: "Well, even if Dad is alive, will he make a full recovery? Will he ever leave the hospital? And if so, in what capacity?" Nevertheless, he set aside what he knew from his experience and prayed—and believed— for my healing. He later told us that as he left the hospital to go home that first night, God reminded him of the song, "You Raise Me Up," leading him to think that God would raise me up and heal me.

Mike and Debbie arrived about 9:30 p.m. Joyce rushed over and gave both of them a big hug, then they sat down with the rest of the group.

"It was a long two hours," Mike acknowledged, referring to the drive he and Debbie had just made. "I was over at the site of the new house, trying to get some work done, when I got the call," he continued. Looking at Matt, he said, "When I saw your number on my cell phone, I thought you were calling to see when we could play golf again. But when you told me you were at the hospital with Mom, I thought something had happened to her. And even when you told me it was Dad, I was sure it couldn't be anything serious. But when I heard you say, 'heart attack' and 'wrecked truck,' my heart went into my throat. I couldn't believe it. I called Debbie and told her, went home to change clothes, and then we headed straight here. All the way down. I kept thinking, 'This can't be happening; not to my dad. He never smokes, never drinks, and he eats as healthy as anyone I ever knew.' And for it to happen after a golf game when I knew that he did not play golf anymore just didn't make sense."

Then Mike thought to himself, "Now that we are here, however, I feel a sense of calm. We are in a family crisis, true, facing something that we have never faced before, but we will all be here together, and I just feel that Dad is going to make it."

Joe and Donna went to my ICU room with my family, and everyone prayed for me. Then, about 10:30 p.m., the assigned nurse told everyone that they had to go home for the night.

Mike and Debbie took Joyce home and would spend the night with her. All day long Joyce had bravely held herself together for everyone else, but on the way home she finally let her emotions come to the surface and she began to just sob. "I'm sorry," she told Mike and Debbie after she composed herself, "but there are times when you have to let it out, get it over with, and then go on."

"That's all right, Mom," Mike reassured her, "you don't have to apologize. We understand."

Joyce got reflective for a moment, then said, "I want Cindy to be here. No matter what the outcome, she needs to be here."

35

"She will be, Mom," Mike said gently. "I'll call early in the morning and make sure."

They got to the house around 11:30 or so, and Joyce began to get ready for bed. As she glanced over at the dresser in our bedroom, she saw my personal items that Mike had gotten from Matt and had left there when they got to the house. The sight of my watch, card case, and cash clip lying there caused her to start sobbing again. She sat down on the edge of the bed and cried out to God. "O God, please let Steve live! It is too soon to bury my husband!"

She suddenly remembered that we had purchased cemetery plots a short time before, and for an instant the thought occurred to her that it must have been God leading us to do so. She immediately rejected and rebuked that thought. She fell on the floor, broken in anguish, and pleaded, "God, please forgive me, for I have sinned! I have not been godly in all of my actions. I have been critical, and I have let little things irritate me. I love my husband, and I cannot imagine him not being here! Lord, he earned two seminary degrees. He reads Your Word continuously, prays about everything, and worships You like few men I have ever seen. You know how much he loves You."

Joyce does not remember all that she said to God during the two hours that she was praying, but when she finally rose to her feet in total exhaustion around 2:00 a.m., she said, "God, I am not finished with Steve yet, and I do not think You are either. Please give us a second chance."

"God, I am Not Finished with Steve Yet, And I Do Not Think You Are Either. Please Give Us a Second Chance."

At that moment, her grandchildren's Veggie Tales® movie of Jonah and the whale came into her mind. She remembered the scene where Jonah is in the belly of the whale, lamenting his trouble, when a heavenly asparagus choir appears and sings a very lively song, "Second Chances." The memory of that scene brought a little smile to her lips. After all of the crying and praying and feeling very, very serious about the situation, it was refreshing to have even a very brief light moment. "Lord," she said out loud, "You are so good."

As Joyce fell into bed she prayed, "Lord, please give me something positive that I can hold onto. It doesn't have to be anything big. All I'm asking for is a small word of encouragement from You."

Joyce closed her eyes, and within ten seconds she heard a still quiet voice say, "Steve will have a wonderful testimony."

Immediately, Joyce sat up in bed and started crying again. "Thank You, Lord! Thank You! This is a *huge* positive thing You have given to me! To have a wonderful testimony means that Steve has to live and he has to have all of his faculties." She was so elated that she could hardly contain herself, but then a serene peace that she had never felt before came over her. It was a peace that went beyond the circumstances, a peace that she should not have had considering what she was going through, a peace that came from knowing that God is God, that He had spoken, and that His word is true. Then, at peace for the first time in hours, she went to sleep.

Endnote
1. Statistics taken from American Heart Association, http://www.heart.org/HEARTORG/ and Heart Rhythm Foundation, http://www.heartrhythmfoundation.org/facts/scd.asp.

Chapter Two

"No Matter the Outcome, God Is Still God"

Cindy pushed the grocery cart ahead of her absentmindedly. She was tired. It had been a long day at work, and she would be glad to get back home. Just a few more items and she would be done. Tomorrow was Friday; she would not be working and she was looking forward to relaxing with her family for the weekend.

However, her reverie was broken as she looked up to see her husband, John, walking rapidly toward her down the grocery store aisle. Her initial surprise turned quickly to concern when she noticed the somber expression on his face. Something was wrong. Something had happened. Her thoughts went immediately to her sons. Was one of them hurt—or worse? She was filled with fear.

When John got close enough, Cindy did not wait for him to speak. "John, what is it?" she asked anxiously. "What's wrong?"

John hesitated, as if he was looking for the right words. This only made Cindy more concerned. "John, what's the matter? Tell me!"

"I just got a call from your brother Matt," John said. "Your father had a heart attack and is in the hospital."

"A heart attack? Dad?" Cindy could not believe what she was hearing. "He has always been one of the healthiest men I know. How could he have had a heart attack?"

"He was playing golf," John continued. "The attack hit just as he was leaving. He smashed his pickup. Somebody pulled him out of the truck, performed CPR, and defibrillated him."

Cindy had enough medical knowledge to understand that this was not good. Her heart froze and she suddenly felt sick. "Is he dead?" she asked, fearing the answer.

John quickly answered, "No, but they rushed him to the hospital, and he is unconscious. That's really all that Matt told me. It's probably all that he knows right now. He asked me to tell you that he will be calling you later."

"John," Cindy said, almost in tears, "can you finish up here? I need to go home."

"Sure, I'll take care of it," John said gently. "You go on home, and I'll see you in a little bit."

Then Cindy left the cart with John and almost ran to the car. The sobs came as Cindy reached her vehicle. She got in, sat for a few moments, dabbing at her eyes, and then started for home, hoping she could drive safely in spite of her tears. All the way home the only thing she could think about was the fact that a person who flatlined and then required CPR and defibrillation usually did not survive. She could not bear the thought that

I was lying unconscious in a hospital, possibly dying—or maybe already dead. Cindy wanted desperately to get home and talk to Matt.

As much as Cindy wanted to learn more about my condition, when Matt phoned not long after Cindy got home, she hesitated to answer because she was not sure she wanted to hear what he had to say. After a few seconds, and bracing herself for the possibility of bad news, she picked up the phone.

"Hi, Matt," she said as calmly as she could manage.

"Hi, Cindy. I suppose John told you about Dad."

Cindy could hear strong emotion in Matt's voice. "Yes, he did. How is Dad?"

"He is unconscious, but alive." A wave of relief swept over Cindy. "They put him in therapeutic hypothermia as soon as they got him to ER and they are getting ready to take him to surgery. That's all I can tell you right now. I will call you later with an update."

After hanging up with Matt, Cindy went to her computer and did a web search for "Hypothermia Therapy." She read about the treatment, as well as the testimony of a man who had been through a similar ordeal and lived. That made her feel a little better, but she still did not sleep very well that night. Several times throughout the night she woke up in a panic, and prayed, "God, please be with Dad. Please don't let him die!"

Joyce woke up at 4:30 Friday morning feeling amazingly refreshed, even though she had only slept about two and a half hours. In those first few minutes of wakefulness, she reflected on all that had happened over the past 24 hours, especially how the staff at Timarron had possessed both the proper equipment and the necessary training to administer the CPR and defibrillation that had kept me alive in those first crucial minutes after my heart attack. The more she thought about it, the more Joyce was convinced that the story should get out. There might be other businesses that would be inspired to get the training and the equipment that could save someone else's life if the need arose.

Then she got an idea. Grabbing her cell phone, Joyce got the phone number for Channel 11 from directory assistance and punched it in. Because it was only a few minutes past 4:30 a.m., she got a recording that told her to punch in the initials of the person she wanted to talk to. The only reporters whose names came to mind were Doug Dunbar and Karen Borta, so she decided to press "D." The voice mail recording that she listened to did not sound like Doug Dunbar, but she left a message anyway. She explained what had happened to me and how grateful she was that the Timarron staff had the training and equipment necessary to save my life, adding also that the doctor had told her that I was alive only because of what they did.

When Joyce ended the call after leaving her message, she had no idea whether or not anything would come of it, but she was confident she had done the right thing. Only time would tell.

Joyce walked into the kitchen to find Mike already up and making coffee. "I didn't sleep much either," he said, anticipating her question.

"Mike," Joyce said, her eyes and voice brimming with excitement, "the Lord spoke to me last night. He said, 'Steve is going to have a wonderful testimony.' Isn't that great? It means that your father is going to live!" They were both encouraged by God's promise.

"It Means that Your Father is Going to Live!"

Mike remembered that he had promised his mother that he would make sure Cindy was here with her mother and her brothers, so while Joyce got ready for their trip to the hospital, he made the call to Pennsylvania. He knew that Cindy would be trying to rest, so he called John's cell phone instead to ask him to make the flight arrangements for Cindy to come down. John was already at work, but he told Mike that he would, of course, book the earliest flight that he could find.

After a fitful night, Cindy had finally fallen asleep not long before sunrise, only to be awakened a couple of hours later by the phone ringing. It was John.

"Your brother Mike just called," he said. "Your mom really wants you to be down there with her and your brothers. She is asking you to come as soon as possible. I will book a flight for you out of Harrisburg and then come home to take you to the airport.

Cindy glanced at the clock. It was 8:30 a.m.. She was exhausted, numb, and barely able to keep her emotions in check. Nevertheless, she got up and threw some clothes into a suitcase. She felt a little better just to be up and doing something. After grabbing a quick bite to eat, she and John left for the airport. Cindy was in a daze the entire drive, her mind swirling with fearful thoughts, speculations, and "what if" scenarios. She found herself on board the airplane with no conscious recollection of how she got there or of having said good-bye to John. As the plane took off, Cindy calmed her mind by taking all her fear and anxiety to the Lord. All the way from Harrisburg, Pennsylvania, to the Dallas/Fort Worth airport, she prayed that I would still be alive when she got there.

A few minutes before Joyce, Mike, and Debbie were ready to leave, Matt and Deborah arrived so that they could all go to the hospital together, but before they left the house, they all held hands and prayed for me. Prayer was their lifeline during this difficult time—and mine too.

That afternoon, Pastor Marcus Brecheen and his wife, Lexa, from Gateway Church came to the hospital to be with Joyce and to pray for me.

We had first met Marcus and Lexa a few years earlier. Both of them have a deep love for the Lord and Joyce and I are both thankful and blessed to know them.

Deborah and Joyce were the only ones in the room with me when Marcus and Lexa arrived; Matt and Mike had left the hospital to pick up Cindy at the airport. After everyone had exchanged greetings and hugs and talked together for a few minutes, they gathered around my hospital bed and Marcus prayed what everyone described later as a "wonderful" prayer. Lexa then prayed for me. In the course of her prayer, the Holy Spirit led her to prophesy about my condition.

"I hear the Lord saying that He will perform a miracle of healing that will be a testimony to your family, and that you will testify to many people of the miracle that God has done."

Joyce could barely contain her excitement at hearing Lexa confirm what God had told her the night before, but somehow she managed to keep quiet until Lexa finished her prayer. Then she could hold it in no longer. "Lexa, your prayer was almost the exact same thing that God said to me last night!"

Then Deb chimed in. "God said the same thing to me! I was praying for Steve this morning and God said, 'Have faith and watch Me work miracles.'"

Isn't God good? Not only did He give Joyce a word to hold onto, but He also confirmed that word through the prayers of other people.

About 4:30 that afternoon, Cindy walked into the waiting room with Mike and Matt. Immediately, she ran to her mother. They hugged each other and cried for a few moments, happy and encouraged just to be together. A short time later, they all went to the ICU. When Cindy saw me lying there in a coma, with all those tubes and machines hooked up to me, she broke down. She said later that the sight of her father, who had always been so strong, lying in a hospital bed unconscious and helpless, perhaps dying, was almost more than she could take. She wanted to get me out of that bed and take me home, but there was nothing she could do and it made her feel completely helpless. Cindy stayed by my bed for the rest of the day, praying that the Lord would bring me back to them. At the same time, she comforted herself with the knowledge that even if He did not restore me to them, I would be with the Lord and would be more than happy there. Cindy was right; she knows her dad.

It was a great comfort to Joyce to have all of her children there with her. Even fortified with God's promise that I would live and have a great testimony, Joyce would have had a very difficult time dealing with everything by herself. In addition to the comfort she received from having her family close, Joyce was further encouraged by the almost continuous parade of pastors and other friends from Gateway who were in and out all day. They shared tears and prayers and moral support and Christian love—everything a community of faith was supposed to be and do.

Another blessing for Joyce was to have a believing and caring nurse on duty. She told me later that the duty nurse was wonderful and assured Joyce that she too was praying for me. That meant so much to Joyce.

Most hospitals place strict limits on how many people can visit a patient in ICU at any one time, as well as how long they can stay. In this case, however, there were no such restrictions. For much of the day, the room was crowded with people standing vigil, holding my hand, and talking to me, Joyce, and other family members. Joyce would rub my shoulder and talk to me and notice on the monitor that my heart rate would go up immediately. The nurse explained that even though I was in a drug-induced coma, my brain would respond to the stimulus of talking and touching. Joyce also brought a CD player into my room and continually played worship music by Gateway's worship team. She knew how much I love praising and worshiping the Lord and was absolutely confident that I would hear the music and worship the Lord in my spirit.

At one point that Friday evening, there were at least a dozen people standing around my bed in the ICU. They were all there for the same reason: to express their love and concern for Joyce and me. As everyone gathered around to pray for me, the Holy Spirit met them and drew them into an anointed time of prayer. Later, Joyce mentioned to the nurse, almost apologetically, about the large number of people in my room. The nurse replied that they normally limit the number to six people at a time, but she also knew that there were times when the family just needs to "take care of things."

Among the crowd of people in my room that day were my younger sister Juanita and her husband Wayne, who had driven down from Vernon in order to be with Joyce. Like me, Juanita had come through a less-than-ideal upbringing but had grown to be a woman who loves the Lord with all her heart. Our "Grandma Foster" helped raise both of us and had been the single most godly influence in our lives growing up. (More on that later.) Nita told Joyce later that it was very difficult to see her "big brother" lying there with tubes going everywhere, but she also said that the Lord gave her a sense of peace that everything was going to be all right. Isn't it amazing how the Holy Spirit was so consistent in what He spoke to people?

At this point I have to say how much we appreciate the prayers and words of encouragement we received from so many of our Christian family at Gateway, as well as from family and friends all across the country. I found out later that there were even people praying for me in Kenya, Thailand, South America, and other places around the world. I thank everyone for their prayers, including those we may not even be aware of. Your prayers made a difference. As James 5:16 assures us, the prayers of the righteous are "powerful and effective" (NIV).

There Were Even People Praying For Me In Kenya, Thailand, South America, and Other Places Around the World.

Joyce and I are especially appreciative of Gene Carter, Jack Abraham, and other pastors and friends from Gateway Church who were so supportive in their prayers and words to us. Gene is the pastor of the over 50, PrimeTime group at Gateway and we have come to appreciate his "always positive" personality and genuine love for the people whom he pastors. Jack Abraham is a key part of the Gateway prayer ministry team, which is where we first met him and Donna. Jack, who has ministered and taught on prayer for more than 20 years, is a great man of prayer and we are forever grateful that he and Donna were there. Jack and Gene both stopped by several times to check on Joyce and me. We feel so blessed to have been the object of such an outpouring of Spirit-led prayer and love from so many people. Thank you, everyone.

At one point during that busy Friday, Joyce was standing beside my bed when her cell phone began to ring. That was another amazing thing about this whole situation: the hospital actually let people use their cell phones inside the ICU. Usually cell phone use is strictly forbidden in such an environment because the cell phone signal potentially could interfere with the hospital equipment.

Joyce picked up her phone, expecting it to be another call from friends or family like the ones she had been getting all day, but was surprised to see "Channel 11" on the display. She had not expected them to return her call so quickly. After introducing herself, the caller from Channel 11 said, "We got your message and would like to talk to you about what happened." Joyce quickly related the story. Then the reporter said, "We have video footage of your husband's pickup against the wall at Timarron and of the ambulance leaving to take him to the hospital. Channel 11 news helicopters respond to most 911 calls, so they were on the scene to record the event as it unfolded. Once they heard that it was a medical emergency and that the victim had had a heart attack, our helicopter left the scene. But we still have the footage. We would like to interview the two of you and run the interview on our news broadcast."

"I'm afraid that my husband is still in critical condition," Joyce told her, "and will not be brought out of his drug-induced coma until Sunday morning. Then there is recovery time after that. My main purpose in calling you was to give you a story illustrating the benefit of a business having the equipment and training to respond to a heart attack."

"I agree with you," the reporter said. "That is a good story, and we will use it, but we would still like to interview both of you at some point, even if we have to wait a while." In an odd sidelight, the Channel 11 reporter told Joyce that her message somehow ended up in the CBS flagship station in New York City. Someone from the New York station had called the Dallas affiliate (Channel 11), saying that it sounded like a great news story and recommended that Channel 11 call Joyce and follow up on it. This really surprised Joyce. To this day, we have no idea how her message wound up in the New York station. We probably will never know.

Friday night everyone left the hospital around 9:30 to go home and get some rest. Our children had been with Joyce all day and they were all exhausted. Mike and Cindy stayed with Joyce that night, and she was able to get a good night's sleep. With Cindy it was another matter. She tried to rest, but did not sleep well knowing that Saturday would be a long day in anticipation of Sunday, when I would be brought out of the coma in order to determine how much damage, if any, had occurred to my heart and brain.

Cindy managed to sleep a little, but woke up at one point early Saturday morning and began praying for me. As she prayed, the Holy Spirit brought to her mind Psalm 23, especially the part that says, "Yea, though I walk through the valley of the shadow of death, I will fear no evil; for You are with me…" (Ps. 23:4). He also led her to Psalm 27:13–14: "I would have lost heart, unless I had believed that I would see the goodness of the Lord in the land of the living. Wait on the Lord; be of good courage, and He will strengthen your heart; wait, I say, on the Lord!" She also found Psalm 56:12–13: "Vows made to You are binding upon me, O God; I will render praises to You, for You have delivered my soul from death. Have You not kept my feet from falling, that I may walk before God in the land of the living?"

These verses were very encouraging to Cindy and she felt that God was telling her that He was taking care of me and that He would completely restore my mind, body, and spirit. After that, Cindy spent most of her time sitting beside my bed, holding my hand, and talking to me. She did not know if I could hear her, but she thought that I did. Saturday, like Friday, saw a lot of visitors to the ICU and my bedside. Cindy was both touched and strengthened by the concern everyone showed and by the words of respect and love they offered.

The main focus on Saturday was initiating the process of slowly warming me up from the hypothermia treatment. Because this procedure would take 24 hours, the plan was to have my body temperature back up to normal by Sunday morning (the third day), then take me off the drugs and wake me up. Since they were very tired and there was nothing they could do at the hospital for the time being, Cindy and Joyce went home to have lunch and rest a little before returning to the hospital to continue their vigil.

Matt, Deborah, and Mike drove to the Timarron Country Club to see if they could talk to the people at the golf course and thank them for all they had done. As they parked and walked up to the clubhouse they could see where my pickup had gone through the flower bed and hit the wall not far from the front door. They saw the tire marks where the tires kept spinning while I was unconscious and not breathing, with my foot on the gas pedal.

As they talked to several people who had been involved and learned more details about what happened, Mike began to realize that everything had to happen exactly the way it did or I would not have survived. In every other scenario that he could think of, I would not have made it. If I had been on the golf course instead of right in front of the clubhouse, they could not have reached me in time. If I had driven past the clubhouse and into the lake on the other side, they would not have been able to get me out of my pickup in time to save me. If I had been on the highway after leaving the club, I would have run off the road and perhaps even taken someone else with me if I had turned into oncoming traffic. Mike concluded that I had a very brief window of opportunity to have a heart attack and live through it. I had to hit the wall right by the front door of the clubhouse, where the equipment and the people trained to use it could get to me quickly and get my heart started again. Mike was amazed to see how God had caused everything to work together to save me, especially the fact that the club had gotten the defibrillation kit and trained the staff in its use only two weeks prior to my heart attack.

God had Caused Everything to Work Together to Save Me.

At Gateway Church, I was the teacher for the Saturday evening PrimeTime class, and Joyce and I had developed relationships with several couples in the class. That Saturday evening, the class met and then decided that rather than have the class, they would come to the hospital to pray for me and to support Joyce. A couple whom we have known for 20 years was there to talk to the class, but they decided to forgo speaking and come to the hospital with the class regulars. As everyone gathered together, and as Joyce saw the concern on their faces, the Holy Spirit prompted her to pray and ask the Lord to give her something to say that would encourage them. He did.

"Steve has spoken many times of Daniel's three friends who were faced with being thrown into Nebuchadnezzar's fiery furnace because they would not bow down and worship his golden image. I'm sure you remember their response to Nebuchadnezzar's threat: 'Our God whom we serve is able to deliver us from the burning fiery furnace, and He will deliver us from your hand, O king. But if not, let it be known to you, O king, that we do not serve your gods, nor will we worship the gold image which you have set up' (Dan. 3:17–18). In other words, whether they lived or died, God was still God and they would serve Him. That is the point that Steve has always emphasized: *No matter the outcome, God is still God.*

"Two nights ago, the Lord told me that Steve would have a wonderful testimony, which meant that he is going to be okay. But even if He were not to heal Steve completely, He is still God."

One of the men looked at her as if he did not fully understand and said, "You seem so positive."

"I am!" Joyce said to him with a smile. "I am trusting in the word that God gave me. Steve is in the fiery furnace right now, but Jesus is with him. He will come through this, and, as a pastor once said, he will not even smell like smoke."

Chapter Three

Awake on the Third Day!

Early Sunday morning, Joyce again was awakened by the phone ringing. She glanced at the display, saw that it was the hospital, and quickly answered.

"Mrs. Graham," the nurse on the other end of the line said, "I'm calling to let you know that we have taken your husband off all the machines that have been monitoring him and have stopped all the medications that were used to keep him asleep. He is breathing on his own and even squeezed my hand on command a few minutes ago, so he is responsive."

"Can he talk?" Joyce asked. "Has he said anything?"

"Barely. He managed to ask, 'What happened?' He is too weak yet to raise his head, so I leaned over and said to him, 'You were playing golf at Timarron Country Club and had a heart attack.'"

A thrill of joy ran over Joyce. I was awake! And I was talking! "How did he respond?" she asked the nurse.

"Well, it was kind of funny," she replied. "His left eyebrow shot up in a high arch (a look my family knows all too well) and managed to whisper, 'But I don't play golf!' Then he fell asleep again."

Joyce hung up the phone almost in a daze. To say that she was excited would be a huge understatement. "Thank You, Lord, for this wonderful news," she prayed as she walked toward the kitchen and almost yelling, "Your Dad's awake!"

Mike was already in the kitchen drinking coffee. "Something interesting happened a few minutes ago, Mom," he said. "I sensed God telling me to go into Dad's office and open his Bible and read Luke 24:7. That's where Jesus says, 'The Son of Man must be delivered into the hands of sinful men, be crucified and on the third day be raised again.' I take it as an encouraging word from God that Dad will recover."

Joyce agreed, and so did Cindy when she walked into the kitchen a few minutes later and Mike told her. The three of them hurriedly ate, got ready, and drove to the hospital as quickly as they could. Cindy said later that they were in such a frenzy to get to the hospital to see me, and her heart was beating so fast, that she thought she was going to have a heart attack herself. As they walked up to the front door of the hospital, Joyce thought, "It is the third day since they put Steve into hypothermia treatment, and now he is back with us." Matt, Deborah, and Brad were waiting for them in the ICU. Together, the six of them walked down to my room.

I was lying in bed with my eyes closed, barely awake, when I heard a soft rustle of noise, which, even in my half-conscious state, I perceived was someone coming into the room. The rustling sound ceased, and after a few moments of silence I heard a gentle, familiar, and wonderful voice speaking to me.

"Honey, it's Joyce."

I opened my eyes to see my lovely wife smiling down at me. I raised my hand and Joyce took hold of it. Then she said, "I love you, Steve."

Speech was still very difficult for me, but I managed to croak out, "I love you too." In my post-heart attack, post-coma muddled state, I did not remember that "I love you too" had been our special saying to each other since before we were married. I tried my feeble best to rise up and kiss her, but I simply did not have the strength. It was a very tender moment for Joyce and she bent down and kissed me. Then, one by one, each of these precious members of my family came to my bedside, took my hand, and told me how much he or she loved me and how thankful he or she was that I was awake.

"What happened?" I asked Joyce. She began to explain it all to me, but as much as I wanted to understand, and as hard as I tried to understand, I simply could not comprehend what she was telling me. I was still too addled by the combined effects of the heart attack, coma, and medications. In addition, I was experiencing constant and considerable chest pain to the point where I was constantly moving, trying to get comfortable. I was also extremely disoriented and I quickly forgot what people told me. As a result, I kept asking the same questions over and over.

The sleep-inducing drugs were wearing off slowly, which meant that I was awake for only short periods of time and then would drift off to sleep again. Each time I woke up I would ask whoever was standing there, "What happened?" and each time the person would tell me that I was playing golf, had a heart attack, wrecked my truck, and "died," but that some of the country club staff had brought me back to life. And each time someone told me the story, I had the same response: I would get a puzzled look on my face and say, "I was playing golf? But I don't play golf. I had a heart attack? But my heart is fine." And every time someone told me that I wrecked my truck, I would say with a pained expression, "I wrecked my truck?" Even after he or she told me that my truck was being repaired, all

I could say was, "I wrecked my truck?" Joyce finally told everyone simply to not tell me about my truck.

Everyone was, of course, overjoyed that I was awake, but I was in intense pain from the CPR compressions and the trauma that I had been through. And since I had been taken off all the medications, I had nothing to numb the pain. Because of my upbringing (which you will learn more of later), I have always had a very high pain tolerance, but the pain I was experiencing in the hospital was almost unbearable for me. I was thrashing and jerking around so much that several times I almost threw myself out of bed. Even something as simple as clearing my throat, which I had to do often after having had breathing tubes, caused me terrific pain.

I was in Intense Pain From the CPR Compressions and The Trauma that I had Been Through.

In addition, as soon as I woke up on Sunday morning, I began to have acute indigestion, resulting in combined hiccups and belches. That was quite an experience! It was hiccup, belch, hiccup, belch, continually. Of course, every time I did either one I experienced tremendous pain in my chest. That is when I would desperately grab the heart-shaped pillow with handles on each side that the hospital had provided, press it to my chest, scream, "Oh God!", throw my legs around wildly, and wait for the pain to subside. Before everything was done, that pillow became a very close friend of mine. One day I held the pillow up in the air and proclaimed, "Look, I have a handle on my heart. Not everyone has a handle on his heart." I love to say things like that even though I know everyone will just politely smile and go on about his or her business.

About mid-morning Sunday a gastro-intestinal specialist was called in to see if he could do anything for my terrible indigestion. After examining me, the gastroenterologist prescribed medication to be given to me intravenously. In talking with Joyce, he revealed that he had once had a heart attack and had experienced severe pain from the CPR compressions he had received. "Does your husband have a history of stomach problems?" he asked Joyce. "Has he ever had this hiccup and belch syndrome before?"

"Steve has had stomach problems most of his life, but he has learned to discipline himself and avoid the foods that cause him problems. Whenever he does have a problem, however, it is usually a big one, what we in the family have come to call a 'Mount St. Helens eruption.'"

All my children quickly agreed and said they had vivid memories of those times.

After I received the medication, my indigestion subsided somewhat, but it did not go away entirely. And then, for some reason I could never explain, they brought me a meal of roast beef with brown gravy, potatoes, and peas! Joyce suggested that I not eat it, but I was very hungry since I had not eaten for three days. I began to consume that meal as fast as I could and surprised everyone by being able to balance peas on my fork even as my shaking hand went from the plate to my mouth. However, after a few bites it came right back up. Joyce held the trash basket close for me to throw up in. As I finished, I looked at Joyce and said, "Well, I guess that food did not need any more anointing and decided to leave." Everybody in the room—the nurse, Matt, Deborah, Cindy, and Joyce—just looked at each other and shook their heads. I think they were encouraged to hear me say such things, which was more like my normal self, even when they knew that I did not know what I was saying or doing.

I fell asleep again, and my family went to lunch. When they got back, they saw that my acute indigestion was accompanied by, as the daily hospital report noted, "intermittent flinging movements of right upper extremity and head." This included violently flinging myself about in the bed, as well as various jerks and facial twitches that mimicked the body movements associated with brain damage. One time in particular when I did this, Deborah and Joyce looked at each other, both thinking the same thing: "This looks like brain damage." Because Joyce was a nurse, and because many of the children Deborah works with have suffered brain damage, they both knew what it looked like.

Looking back, Joyce realizes now that this was a temptation to lose her faith by accepting what she saw rather than holding onto the word that God had given her. However, the Holy Spirit strengthened her faith, enabling her to affirm, "God said that Steve will have a wonderful testimony. That means that he will recover and will not have brain damage. What we are seeing, therefore, must be a reaction to one or more of the medications he has been given."

"He Will Recover and Will Not Have Brain Damage."

Sunday was a day of elation at seeing me awake, but also a day of deep concern as my family watched me suffer the effects of the severe chest pain, the acute indigestion, and the muscle spasms and facial twitches that so much looked like brain damage. They felt every pain with me, and by the end of the day they were physically and mentally exhausted. In the early evening, thinking that the worst was over, Mike drove back to his home and the rest of my family also went home to get some rest.

About 9:30 that night, Joyce got a call from Dr. Moustapha. Earlier Joyce had hurt her back, and she had just taken a muscle relaxant to relieve the severe pain so she could rest. The medicine had just kicked in when she got the call. Since she could not stand up, she sat down on the floor to talk to the doctor.

"Mrs. Graham," he said, "your husband's chest pain is so bad that I am concerned that he might be having another heart attack, or that something else might be wrong. I would like to do another MRI and I need your permission."

"Of course," Joyce said. "Do whatever you need to do."

Joyce knew that she was in no condition to drive and Cindy did not feel comfortable driving, so she called Matt and asked him to take them back to the hospital. Matt agreed, of course, and when he arrived at the house, Joyce and Cindy climbed into his car and off they went again.

By the time they got to the hospital the doctor had completed the MRI and a nurse reported that he did not find any heart problem. They had also done a chest X-ray to see if I had any broken or cracked ribs, but saw no sign of any. They concluded that I probably had separated ribs, which certainly would cause the intense chest pain I was experiencing. I had suffered from separated ribs once before, so Joyce knew how much pain they can cause. Armed with that news, Joyce and the others checked in on me, saw that I was resting, and went back home to try, finally, to get some rest themselves.

When Joyce and Cindy got home there was a message on the phone from Linda Kipley. Linda and her husband Kip have been close friends of ours, a brother and sister in the Lord, for more than 30 years. Joyce was excited to hear Linda's voice. She knew that Kip and Linda had gone to Thailand on a church mission trip and assumed at first that they did not know about what had happened to me. Linda's message, however, said that Cindy's husband, John, had sent them an email telling them all about what had happened, but she and Kip had not been able to receive emails until they got back to Ubon. Linda said that Kip had turned white when he read the email and, like everyone else, could hardly believe that this had happened to me. Linda said that as soon as Kip told her what was in the email, she knew she had to call Joyce.

Kip and Linda explained the situation to the missionary couple they were staying with, and the four of them immediately joined in prayer for my recovery. The missionaries then told Kip and Linda that they would send the word out to all of the churches in Thailand that they were associated with and ask them also to pray for me.

Kip has come through four operations to be completely free from cancer. One of those operations was one of the most intense spiritual battles that we have ever been through as we knew that his life was in the balance. Because of their own experience, Kip and Linda knew the reality of praying for someone in an emergency situation and I know that they felt it personally as they prayed for me and contacted others to ask them to pray with them.

The missionary couple also graciously allowed Linda to use their phone to call Joyce. This was extremely gracious on their part because Linda's message was a long one, and an international call all the way from Thailand was not cheap. But close friends stand with you in a crisis no matter where they are. Linda had called immediately after receiving the email from John to let us know that they were praying with us and that the congregations in Thailand were praying with us too. After many other reassurances Linda said that they were on their way back home and would call again as soon as they arrived. It was so good for Joyce to hear from Linda and know that her and Kip's loving support transcended the physical distance between us. Linda's encouraging words were a fitting way to wind down from all that had taken place on that Sunday, the "third day."

Chapter Four

"Steve Is a Miracle"

Monday morning at 6:30, Joyce again woke up to a phone call from the hospital and again it was Dr. Moustapha. As soon as she heard his voice, Joyce felt a surge of alarm because she knew that the doctor himself would not have called unless there was a problem.

"Mrs. Graham," he began, "I am still concerned about the intense level of pain that Steve is experiencing. Even morphine is not reducing it. I would like to do another heart catheterization just to verify with my own eyes that there is no other blockage or any problems with the stent."

"Of course you have my permission, Doctor," Joyce said, "but let me ask you this: Can you do something about the muscle spasms Steve is having?"

"I am concerned about that as well," Dr. Moustapha replied, "and I have requested consultation with a neurologist."

By the time Joyce and Cindy got to the hospital that morning, they had already done the heart catheterization and the doctor told them that everything looked great. This was another "Praise God!" moment. However, they still spent the better part of the day trying to keep me as comfortable as possible. All day long I kept jerking and flinging myself from side to side so violently that Joyce spent most of her time just trying to keep me covered up.

About 6:00 that evening the neurologist came into the room to talk to Joyce.

Earlier in the day, he had ordered a brain scan and had now come to discuss the results.

"I have good news, Mrs. Graham," he said. "I have examined Steve's brain scan closely and have found no evidence of any brain damage or any other adverse effects from his cardiac arrest. Once I saw that his scan was clear, I did some research and discovered that the medication that Steve has been given for his stomach problem can, in very rare instances, cause the muscle spasms, twitches, jerks, and other involuntary movements we have been seeing. As soon as I learned that, I ordered his stomach medication stopped. Considering the severity of Steve's heart attack, the fact that he survived at all, much less survived with no brain damage or other adverse effects, is truly remarkable. As far as I am concerned, Steve is a miracle."

"He certainly is," Joyce agreed. Then she said, "Doctor, can you order some kind of pain medicine for Steve that will help him sleep?" Because of my severe pain and the fact that I had been asleep for three solid days, I had hardly slept at all Sunday night or Monday.

The neurologist smiled and said, "I already have."

"Thank you, Doctor. I really appreciate everything you have done."

After the doctor left the room, everybody hugged each other, overjoyed at the news he had given them. A clear brain scan! No brain damage or any other adverse effects!

A short time later, a nurse came in and injected the prescribed pain medicine into my IV. "This will put him to sleep," she said. Sure enough, within minutes after receiving the medication, I fell fast asleep for the first time in almost 24 hours. My family was greatly relieved that I was finally able to relax.

With my successful resuscitation from the drug-induced coma and the discovery that I had suffered no permanent damage, the main crisis had passed, but I still faced a long road to full restoration of health. The immediate days that followed were filled with the process of my continuing recovery from the treatments and medications that had been necessary to keep me alive. Slowly, I began to regain some of my strength; not much, but some. I appeared coherent and would even carry on conversations with people who were there, but I would not remember them a few minutes later. I do not remember this, but some of our friends insist that one day when they came in to pray for me, I prayed for them and even gave them an encouraging word from the Lord.

I Still Faced a Long Road to Full Restoration of Health.

However, there were definite signs that I was not "fully there" yet. One time I introduced our children to Jack and Donna Abraham three times during the same conversation. Another time, I asked Wes Pool during one of his visits if Mickey Mantle had played that day. (Mickey retired in 1968 and died in 1995.) Then there was the time when Cindy, Deborah, and Joyce came into the room and I called out loudly, "Look! I am being visited by three beautiful women. Not many men get to be visited by three beautiful women." I make it a habit to try to be complimentary, but this was a little out of character for me.

Cindy told me later that doctors would come into the room, look me over, and say, "Mr. Graham, you are a miracle." They rarely saw such a positive outcome for a heart attack victim in such serious condition as I was when I was brought in that Thursday afternoon. I think the heart doctor summed it up best when he said, "Mr. Graham, it is highly unlikely that this happened to you, and it is a miracle that you survived with no damage." That pretty much says it all.

To this day, I do not remember any of my hospital stay; an aftereffect, I suppose, of my cardiac arrest, drug-induced coma, and all the medications I received. But everyone assures me that I continued to make progress, and I guess they are right because here I am today, restored to full health and full capacity and possessing all my faculties (although some of my friends may doubt this last one!). With regard to my brain scan, I now like to tell people (borrowing a story from Dizzy Dean, the old-time baseball player), that they took a scan of my brain and the report said, "Scan of Steve Graham's brain shows nothing!"

On Tuesday morning, November 4, 2008, Joyce was awakened by the phone, just as she had been for the last several mornings. When she saw that the call came from Baylor Grapevine Hospital, her first thought was, "Oh no, what now?" It was a reasonable question, in light of the fact that each previous early morning call had been from a doctor requesting her okay for some procedure he needed to perform on me.

Cautiously, Joyce picked up the phone. Instead of the formal, businesslike tone of a doctor, however, she heard a very raspy voice say, "Hey, babe, do you know where I am?"

Joyce's heart skipped a beat to hear my voice, but she quickly recovered. "Yes, dear," she answered. "Do you know where you are?"

Then she heard me say, in what she described as a very pitiful tone, "The hospital?"

"Yes, dear, and we will be up there shortly to see you. Matt and Brad were with you last night until the hospital made them leave. Do you remember that?"

"No, I don't," I said.

Hearing the confusion in my voice, Joyce thought, "Bless his heart, he woke up thinking we did not even know he was in the hospital."

A few minutes later, Joyce was talking to Cindy about the conversation she had with me. "I just got a call from your father," she told Cindy. "He sounded as though he was aware enough to know he was in the hospital, but was afraid that we did not know he was there."

"I feel bad for Dad, waking up in a strange place with none of us there," Cindy said. She was thoughtful for a few moments, then continued, "What I am wondering is how in the world Dad got hold of a telephone."

Joyce nodded. "I was wondering the same thing."

Joyce and Cindy spent most of the day at the hospital with me, as often as they were allowed into my room. The nursing staff had me up walking around the nurses' station with a belt around my waist and a nurse holding onto the back of the belt to keep me as steady as she could. However, even with the nurse's help I was so weak I could only take baby steps. Between walks I spent most of the day sitting in the chair that was in my room. I kept telling Joyce, "I can't believe how weak I am."

Matt and Brad came to the hospital to stay with me and to try and convince their mother and sister to go home and get some needed rest. As thankful as they were in the knowledge that I was going to make it and not have any brain or heart damage, the stress of the past several days had nonetheless taken their toll on Joyce and Cindy. "Go home and get some sleep," Brad and Matt told them. "We'll stay with Dad until visiting hours are over." Since it was a 45-minute drive home, Joyce and Cindy agreed.

It was election day. After getting home and changing their clothes, Joyce and Cindy sat and talked quietly together about all that had taken place. Their plan was to relax and watch the election results. Within a few minutes of turning on the TV, however, they both fell fast asleep.

The jangling of the phone abruptly woke them both. They looked at each other, wide-eyed, both thinking the same thing: "Oh no, what is the hospital calling about now? What do they want this time?" It was not the hospital, however, but John, Cindy's husband, calling to tell them that the presidential election had been called and that we had a new president. Weariness and being awakened suddenly from a deep sleep brought their feelings to the surface. Cindy fell onto the love seat, crying, and Joyce realized just how raw their nerves were from all that they had been through. Once they were fully awake and had composed themselves, they watched President-elect Barack Obama give his acceptance speech. Afterwards, they finally went to bed.

Lying in bed, unable to sleep right away, Joyce began reflecting on how things happen in our lives, but the world goes on. Presidents are elected; babies are born; people die; and the world keeps going. "Steve could have died," she thought, "and we would have kept right on living and doing what we had to do to deal with losing someone we loved so much. It would be very hard and we could do it only by focusing on Christ and not on our loss. Thankfully, Steve did not die. Heavenly Father, You have been with us through all that we have had to go through, and by Your grace and mercy, life will go on. As small and insignificant as I am in this world, You heard me. Your Holy Spirit gave me comfort in my time of trouble and now we are going on. You are indeed an awesome God." In the restfulness of these thoughts, Joyce finally fell asleep.

"By Your Grace and Mercy, Life Will Go On."

At 7:30 the next morning, Joyce received another phone call. This time the raspy voice on the line asked her to bring my Bible, my glasses, my card case, my money clip, and my watch. Joyce understood why I wanted my Bible and glasses, but she knew that I had no real use for the other things I had asked for. Nevertheless, when she and Cindy came to the hospital, she brought everything that I had requested. They walked into my room to find me sitting up in bed with a clipboard and pencil. I immediately asked, "Did you bring my Bible?" Joyce answered yes, and with a great sweeping motion of my hand I checked off the first item on the list that I had made. Then, in a loud voice I said, "Check." I then repeated this procedure for each item on the list.

When I had completed checking off all of the items on my list, Cindy turned to Joyce and said, "He's back!"

Joyce got hold of my "check list" later; it was completely illegible to the point where even I could not read it. At the time, however, I apparently knew exactly what it said. Joyce then asked the nurse not to give me a clipboard or pencil again.

Cindy did not really want to leave, but she had been there a week already. And since I was coming around and everyone knew that I was going to make it, she went back home. She said later that at various times the whole ordeal had been surreal, frightening, amazing, and uplifting. During the flight home, she reflected on how much she and her brothers had come together during this time of crisis, how much strength God had given them, how God had spoken to each of them in a different way, how the experience had drawn them closer, and what good and capable men her brothers had become. It made her realize the strength that God gives us in our times of need and that He really does love us and shows us mercy. It renewed her faith and reminded her that she can lean on Him when she feels as though she can't take another step. The whole experience made her realize that it is in times like this that we learn our most valuable lessons from God.

She was reminded that it is in the difficult times that we truly learn of God's faithfulness, love, and mercy that go beyond our natural ability to understand. It is in those times when the Holy Spirit speaks to our spirits and writes God's truth on our hearts. When we look back at the experience, we understand that what we went through was really for our good.

My experience was no different, and although I do not yet understand all that God has done and will do through it, I am thankful for all that has and will take place. We have experienced some very difficult times in our life, but we have come to see how faithful God was through them all.

Even today I do not remember anything from just before that fateful golf game to the day I went home from the hospital, and little detail about the next couple of weeks. That is fine with me because I do remember that it was not the most comfortable time I have ever had. Like most men, when I first came home from the hospital I thought I could do more than I actually could do because I did not realize how weak I still was. I still had a lot of pain and soreness in my chest and still had to grab my heart pillow every time I coughed or sneezed or moved the wrong way. This resulted in my sleeping in my chair for a few minutes at a time and then not being able to sleep at night because of the pain that I had when I tried to lie down. Joyce also did not sleep much because she was checking on me every few minutes (well, it seemed like it anyway). Fortunately for me, she was always there to remind me that I was not able to do all that I wanted to do.

One time I got up out of my chair and went into the garage where my workbench, tools, and home repair supplies are. To make sure that I was not going to try to work on something, Joyce came out right behind me. "And just what do you think you are doing in the garage?" she demanded.

Somewhat sheepishly, I replied, "I just wanted to be here for a few minutes to look at everything." I knew that was not completely true, so I 'fessed up. "Actually, I know I got up and walked in here, but now I cannot remember why." This was another example of my not being fully recovered but thinking that I was.

I was able to hold it together enough for a Channel 11 reporter and cameraman to come to our house just three days after I got out of the hospital. They came to film an interview with us concerning my cardiac arrest and the importance of the Timarron employees' having the defibrillator unit and knowing how to use it. Later that same evening, Joyce and I watched the broadcast showing the film they had taken at Timarron on the day of the incident and the interview they did with us in a news clip they titled, "Defibrillator Kit." I was very glad that Channel 11 gave us a DVD of the broadcast. Seeing the pictures of my pickup against the retaining wall, the emergency vehicle at the scene, and the interviews that they did with the Timarron employees gave us tangible evidence that it really did happen. Needless to say, we have watched it many times.

After several weeks of slowly regaining some of my strength, and with the pain subsiding, I was able to start rehab at Baylor Grapevine heart rehab center. For the first several sessions Joyce had to drive me, but when I was allowed to drive again, I went by myself. What a great feeling that was, to finally have some independence again and be able to do some things for myself! I did have to promise Joyce that I would call her when I got to the rehab center and again when I left to come home. She said that she wasn't worried but just wanted to make sure I made it okay.

What a Great Feeling that Was, to Finally Have Some Independence Again!

I cannot say enough about the care and encouragement I received from the rehab nurses. They knew exactly what they were doing and tried their best to make sure everyone who was there for rehab did what they were supposed to do. During the rehab sessions, I met several other men who were also there for heart rehab. One of them was not only doing rehab after bypass surgery, but also going through a difficult time with his son, trying to decide how best to help his son get off drugs and on the path to his own rehab. This gave me the opportunity to share some personal insights into his situation, to let him know of God's faithfulness in my life, including my most recent experience, and to tell him that I would be praying with him to see his son restored.

Another man also in rehab after heart surgery mentioned that his wife was in the hospital. The doctor had told her that she could go home for the Christmas holiday if she was able to eat and get some nourishment, which she was not able to do at that time. We offered up a prayer for her on Friday, and on Monday he told me that she had experienced a turnaround and would be going home for Christmas.

Sometime later, I was checking in one morning at the same time a lady recovering from a heart attack was checking in. She was having a difficult time but was there to try to start her rehab. I had just started my session on the treadmill when I looked up to see the nurses racing to take care of this lady, who had been working out on one of the other machines but was now obviously in distress. Two nurses got to her quickly and while they were working on her I stood by them and prayed for her and the nurses. I found out later that she had suffered a heart attack while she was on the machine, but made a good recovery.

By setting higher goals each week for each machine I was able to exceed the expected goals by the end of the 36-session program. When I "graduated" (they actually have a cap and gown, play music, and take your picture with the nurses), I told all of the nurses how much I appreciated all that they had helped me do. "I know you get paid for what you do," I told them, "but I also know that this is more than just a job for you. It requires you to give your very best and to show a lot of love to your patients. That is what you did for me and everyone else here. Thank you, and may the Lord bless you."

At my first follow-up visit to the heart doctor, he told me that my heart was up to about 70% capacity. After continuing workouts at home, however, my June follow-up visit produced a "clean bill of health" with my heart working at full capacity and no damage from the cardiac arrest! What a mighty God we serve!

Oh, there is one more thing. Because the accident report that the investigating officer completed said that my accident occurred because I "blacked out," the state of Texas informed me that I would have to have my heart doctor complete a questionnaire that would be reviewed by a committee of doctors. The committee would then determine whether I could keep my driver's license or whether I would have to go before a justice of peace and let him hear the facts and make the decision. I have had my driver's license since I was 14 and it is very dear to me, so I wanted to get this taken care of as quickly as possible. I was not entirely happy with this process, but it was Texas law, so I followed the rules and did get to keep my driver's license.

The next time I went to rehab I stopped by Dr. Moustapha's office and explained to his nurse that I needed the doctor to complete the questionnaire and mail it to the state. When I told her that the investigating officer had indicated "blacked out" on his report as the reason for my accident, she responded, "You didn't black out; you died!"

"You Didn't Black Out; You Died!"

I thought about that for a moment. It was true. Yes, I did die, but God brought me back to life. I had experienced an extraordinary event with extraordinary results. My heart had stopped and I had died, but God had ordained that it happen in the right place, at the right time, with the right people to bring me back to life and have me survive with no heart damage and no brain damage. How thankful I am that God does extraordinary things in the lives of ordinary people.

Call upon Me in the day of trouble; I will deliver you, and you shall glorify Me

PSALM 50:15

Be strong and of good courage, do not fear nor be afraid of them; for the Lord your God, He is the One who goes with you. He will not leave you nor forsake you

DEUTERONOMY 31:6 (SEE ALSO MATTHEW 28:20.)

...I am the resurrection and the life. He who believes in Me, though he may die, he shall live. And whoever lives and believes in Me shall never die...

JOHN 11:25–26

Part Two

An Extraordinary Journey

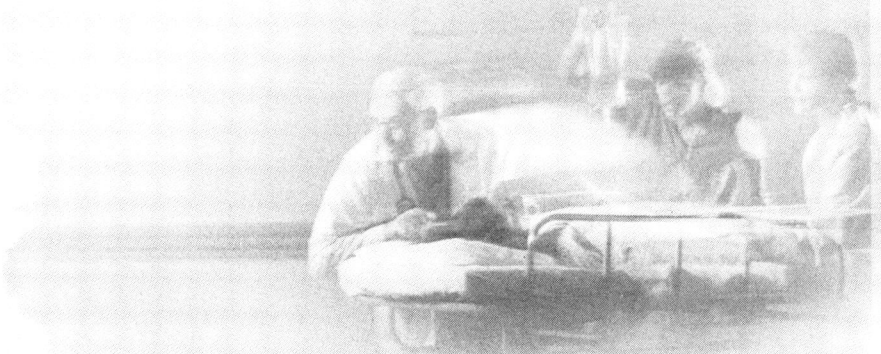

Introduction

What do you do after your heart has stopped beating, you have stopped breathing, you have turned blue, you have been revived, and finally you wake up in the hospital with no memory of what has happened? Well, after I made sure Joyce knew where I was and I somewhat understood what had happened, I began to thank God for everything, including the cardiac arrest and for the good that I knew would come out of it. Each time we have had a traumatic experience of some kind, He has always been faithful to show us more of Himself and to speak truth into our lives that we might come to know Him more. So naturally, after having my heart stop and being brought back to life, my question was, "Lord, what are You saying to us through this experience? What do You want us to see?"

In answer to my prayer, the Lord said, "Steve, I first want you to remember the great love and faithfulness that I have extended to you and Joyce through these many years." The Holy Spirit then took me back over our many years of walking with Him. He reminded me of the many times the Lord had shown Himself faithful to us by showing us His truth through difficult situations that we faced and how He came to show us more of Himself through them.

In the pages that follow, I will share briefly some of the recollections that went through my mind as I talked with the Lord while lying in my hospital bed and later as I was recovering at home. (I started to say, "raced" through my mind, but "crawling" would be a more accurate term.) Each one of these recollections, as well as so many others that I will not mention, is a separate story full of marvelous details of God's loving hand at work. Here, however, I will take the time to mention only the highlights of a few to illustrate His love and faithfulness over these many years. Romans 8:29 says that those who are His, "He also predestined to be conformed to the image of His Son, that He might be the firstborn among many brethren." As you read these stories and the summary comments I make concerning the primary things that we learned through our experiences, I hope you will see that our walk with the Lord is a lifetime process of coming to know Him more, thus becoming more like Him as we are transformed from our fallen nature into the nature of Christ by the Father's love through the working of the Holy Spirit.

Christ trained His disciples through His teaching of the truth of God's Word, through their experiences with Him, and through their times of close fellowship with Him. He does the same with us. As the Holy Spirit opens the eyes of our understanding, He reveals Christ to us in His Word, from the first chapter to the last. We come to see Him and know Him and understand His majesty, His greatness, His holiness, His love, His mercy, His compassion, and His preeminence in all things as He ever leads us through the difficulties and triumphs that we encounter in this life. We come to see Him and know Him more as He grants us those times of close fellowship and communion with Him. Through this lifetime process we come to love Him above all things and we come to understand that each element of the process is necessary, that they are all in His perfect timing, and that they all work together for our ultimate, eternal good.

As you read these stories and my comments, please keep in mind that what we came to understand we learned after we encountered God in the midst of the experience and after He opened the eyes of our understanding to His Word. Only then did we comprehend the truth of what He was teaching us. During each experience we usually were trying just to make our way through the darkness until we found His guiding light. In the difficulties and the triumphs everything in our nature was pulling us down, and it was only His loving hand that reached down and lifted us up to be with Him and to see from His perspective as He went with us through each experience.

Also, please understand that my comments about these experiences are only one aspect of what we learned or what God confirmed to us in prayer and fellowship with Him. As with all parts of this book, they are not intended to be a dissertation or otherwise deep discussion of each element of what we came to see; rather, they simply share how great God is, even when we did not recognize it at the time. They are simply brief statements of what we learned while we were in the midst of an experience or what we later saw as we looked back at the outcome. I pray that you will see that the answers we needed or the solution to our problem or what He was teaching us or the peace that we had did not come from focusing on the crisis or the triumph but from focusing on Christ. We also pray that God will use our experiences to help you on your own journey of discovering the joy of trusting God in all things.

Let me preface my sharing of these experiences by saying that I am very aware of our scriptural responsibility to honor all authority, as Scripture clearly tells us that all authority is from God (see Rom. 13) and is ultimately accountable to God. I am also aware that Titus 3:1–2 tells us that we are "to be subject to rulers and authorities" and "to speak evil of no one." To do otherwise is to dishonor God and feed our natural inclination to rebel against authority. I am also aware of His command to honor our parents lest we be those who honor God with our lips but in our hearts are far from Him (read Matthew 15). Please do not read this as an attempt either to display the faults of others or to blame them for our troubles in order to make ourselves look better. Although this is a natural and easy thing to do, it is an approach that is contrary to God. Please read what I have said as a humble attempt to testify of God's goodness and faithfulness as He has worked in our lives, showing us His love and more of who He is. Please read it as our personal testimony given from a heart full of love for Him, and as our prayer to Him to help others see that it is in Christ alone that we have hope for the future regardless of our past, present, or future experiences.

> *Oh, give thanks to the Lord! Call upon His name; make known His deeds among the peoples! Sing to Him, sing psalms to Him; talk of all His wondrous works! Glory in His holy name; let the hearts of those rejoice who seek the Lord! Seek the Lord and His strength; seek His face evermore! Remember His marvelous works which He has done, His wonders, and the judgments of His mouth*
>
> 1 CHRONICLES 16:8–12

Chapter Five

With Us From the Beginning

To say that we started this journey under less than ideal circumstances would probably be an understatement. Joyce was born in a one-bedroom house that had no heating, on a day when a winter storm was blowing outside. In order to ensure that her newborn daughter stayed warm, Joyce's mother kept her in bed with her all day. By contrast, I was born in a hospital in the north Texas town where my maternal grandparents lived. When I was released from the hospital, however, my parents took me across the Red River to a farmhouse in southern Oklahoma where they had nailed newspapers on the walls in an attempt to keep the cold wind from blowing through the house. This was the same house where one night my mother mistakenly left a loaf of bread on the table, only to discover the next morning that rats had eaten all of the bread but left the bread wrapper standing as if the bread was still in it. My parents had an old car that they had to push down the hill next to the house to get started. I think that by most human standards this was not the best way for either Joyce or me to begin life.

Joyce's father was a good man who always worked hard for his family, but he was not a "professing Christian." Her mother took her to church and Sunday school in her early years and she still remembers lessons she learned there. However, the only religious heritage she can remember came from her maternal grandmother, who was a devout member of a hard-line, works-based denomination. Joyce remembers her as someone who regularly went to church but was very stern and not a very happy person. She does not remember any Christians in her father's family and only the women in her mother's family attended church. But God used even this thin line of connection to give Joyce at an early age a sensitivity to Him that would connect her to His grace throughout her life and would be a key part of God's speaking to us in critical points of our marriage.

In my early childhood years my father had to stop farming after a hailstorm ruined the crop he was counting on to get us through to the next year. Eventually he worked his way to owning two bars in southern Oklahoma. My grandfather Graham owned another bar in a nearby town. Mine was a life of being raised in the midst of dysfunctional, codependent, enabling relationships; anger; adultery; alcohol; smoking; and people driven by the basest of desires. Childhood memories include being with my mother as she drove to motels to confront my father and, at age nine or so, being sent in to beg my father, who was semi-conscious on the couch, not to leave us. I remember living in fear of severe physical punishment for things I did wrong, but with a strange mixture of love (as he knew it) from a father who was raised in even worse conditions.

At age 12 or so, my father became the head of his family of seven siblings when my grandfather left. Later, he came to the point of holding a gun to his father's head, wanting to kill him. Thankfully, he did not pull the trigger. One of my most vivid memories of those early years is being frozen in fear as I watched my grandfather Graham beating my grandmother (his second wife) as my aunts stood by screaming and not being able to do anything about it. These and many other incidents that need not and should not be mentioned were part of a lifestyle that was, to say the least, not conducive to knowing anything about God, much less "seeking" to know anything about Him. It has, therefore, always been a marvel to me that I did not follow that lifestyle that leads to ultimate destruction, but instead, God, by His grace alone, put me on a path that led me to Him.

God's saving grace and mercy included putting godly people in my life at times and occasions when I needed His correction or redirection. It also included my father having a conversion experience in a denominational church, getting a lay minister's license, and, while still holding a secular job, being the pastor of three rural congregations that could not afford a full-time pastor. Thus, during my high school years, God introduced me to church life and provided me with the discipline of being a "preacher's son" to keep me from many things I probably otherwise would have done. I did not really understand much about what was going on; nor did I actually know God, but during this time God began to give me a respect for Him, His Word, His Church, and His people and introduced me to the idea of living a life of prayer and faith. My understanding was, of course, embryonic, imperfect, and limited by my narrow perspective, but the seeds were planted.

Unfortunately, shortly after I graduated from high school my father succumbed to the temptations of his fleshly desires and went back to his old way of life. Perhaps you can imagine how traumatic and devastating this was for me, how it fanned the flames of anger and resentment in me toward my father that had somewhat died down during his church years. However, to keep things somewhat in sequence, I will leave until later the story of how I finally came to understand the bondage of resentment that I lived in for many years, as well as the forgiveness that was necessary to release me from that bondage. I thought that I could bury my anger and resentment inside, but God, in His grace and mercy, showed me how absolutely essential the forgiveness was that released me and allowed me to go on with Him.

Did my upbringing leave scars and produce problems that would take years of growth in Christ to overcome? Do I pray that men and women would understand how devastating adultery, alcohol, anger, tobacco, a "me first and children last" mentality, and other such self-focused destructive actions and mindsets are to their children? Do I pray that parents would understand their responsibilities and the effect that their attitudes and actions have on their children? Do I pray for children who have been or are being sacrificed upon the altar of their parents' self-indulgence? Of course I do. But by God's grace, I do not blame my father or my grandfather for the issues that I had to work through later in my life. That would be the easy course to follow and an easy excuse for not taking personal responsibility to address core issues that could only be dealt with in Christ. They were who they were, and God knew the family that I would be born into. He knew how I would be raised and how He would use that experience to show me the truth of His love and mercy and grace in Christ, through the Holy Spirit.

By God's Grace, I do Not Blame My Father or My Grandfather for the Issues that I had to Work Through Later in My Life.

As He started me on the process of growing in my knowledge of and relationship with Him, I am thankful that I did not know enough about religious culture to understand that we were supposed to relate to God only through the particular religious organizational structure that we belonged to and by following that organization's prescribed methods, rules, and regulations. I am thankful that I did not know that God was a Father in name only, or that we were not supposed to have two-way conversations with Him, or that we could only hear from Him by reading specified portions of the Bible. Please hear me when I say that I would never say anything negative about the Bible or of our need to reverence the revealed Word of God. The Bible is His "God-breathed" Word to us. It is the primary source of His life-giving instruction for our walk with Him. The Spirit-enlightened study of His Word is absolutely essential to our walk with God, as it reveals Christ to us and consequently reveals God's truth to us. It is where we see His nature. It is the standard by which we measure and balance life as the Holy Spirit leads us to see who God is, who we are in relation to God, and, therefore, how much we have been forgiven. It reveals Him as the One who created and sustains all things and who rules and reigns over all things. It reveals His absolute holiness and our nature of absolute rebellion against His absolute authority and the absolute consequences of that rebellion. But then it reveals His provision of forgiveness of our rebellion in the sacrifice of our Lord Jesus Christ and His salvation for us no matter how contrary we are at the time. His truth has been once and forever revealed in His Word and much error has come when people set aside the Word to find self-focused direction from other sources.

I love God's Word beyond my ability to express, and it is my constant companion. But He is the true Father who, through His presence with and in us by the Holy Spirit, speaks to His children primarily through His Word, but also through His servants' teaching and preaching Christ, and in our discovering Christ through our life-changing experiences. His chosen people are His sons and daughters no matter where they are or what they are doing. He loves us with a love that surpasses understanding and we are called to walk with Him and relate to Him as a son or daughter. Therefore, I have never understood how we can have an intimate personal relationship with Him if we can only communicate with Him through someone else or through some formal ritual or through prescribed reading. Can you imagine what a parent-child relationship or a husband-wife relationship would be like or what a relationship between friends would be like if that was the only way we could relate?

All I knew at the beginning of my walk with God was that He loved me and that we have close fellowship and two-way communication with those who truly love us and whom we love in return. How thankful I am that even from the beginning, when God first caused me to know and care that He was there, as childlike and limited as that knowing and caring was at the time, He gave me a heart to relate to Him in an intimate and personal way.

As you will see from the examples in the following chapters, we came to understand that God is a faithful Father who knows what we need before we ask and who always directs us, teaches us, and provides for us out of His everlasting, unconditional love. In 1 John, the apostle writes to children, young men, and fathers, laying foundations of truth that will encourage them in their lifelong journey to know Christ. As little children we are given what we need to grow and become stronger. As young men He trains us for the battles that we face as we learn to focus on Him, trust in Him alone, and thereby achieve victory. As fathers, we have matured in our relationship with God and the focus of our desire is to know Him more. Each day we long to be more like Christ and we long to be with Christ. It is a lifetime journey of coming from just knowing that He is, of just knowing about Him, to a relationship of truly knowing Him and seeking to please Him in every thought, every word, and every deed.

Starting where we did, I am glad that coming to know God is a lifetime process because Joyce and I had a lot to learn and a lot to change. As with everything else, we interpret images and concepts of God through the filter of our fallen human nature, which always leads us to a misinterpretation and false understanding of their true meaning. For example, when we hear that God is our Father, we filter that image through our human understanding and our human experience, leaving us with an imperfect and unclear understanding of His true Fatherhood. Even the best of fathers are only types and shadows of our true Father and thus cannot give us a completely clear picture of Him. Having a less than ideal upbringing by fathers who had their own issues to deal with makes it even more difficult to see the truth. Whether that upbringing was in a home without God or in a home with a church-going pharisaical legalist, the Holy Spirit must open our hearts and minds to the truth of Scripture before we can see the truth of our heavenly Father. Considering our preconceived ideas—and viewing our life experiences through that same filter—we conclude either that God is a harsh, uncaring, distant demigod who has left us to flounder on our own or that He is a benevolent grandfather handing out candy each time we decide to visit Him. But by the love, mercy, and grace of God, the Holy Spirit leads us to see the truth of Christ, enabling us to see and understand God's true Fatherhood.

I am Glad that Coming to Know God is a Lifetime Process Because Joyce and I had a Lot to Learn and a Lot to Change.

That understanding is revealed to us in our Lord Jesus Christ. When we see Christ we see both His perfect representation *of* the Father (perfect love), and His perfect example of our relationship *with* the Father (perfect obedience). In John 12:49, Christ said, "For I have not spoken on My own authority; but the Father who sent Me gave Me a command, what I should say and what I should speak." A little later He said, "Do you not believe that I am in the Father, and the Father in Me? The words that I speak to you I do not speak on My own authority; but the Father who dwells in Me does the works" (John 14:10). Out of His oneness with the Father, Christ was the perfect representation of the Father, and it is only in Christ that we see the Father. It is only in Christ that we come to the Father; it is only in Christ that we see the Son's relationship to the Father; it is only in Christ that we have fellowship with the Father. Jesus said in John 14:6–7, "I am the way, the truth, and the life. No one comes to the Father except through Me. If you had known Me, you would know My Father also; and from now on you know Him and have seen Him."

As it is only in Christ that we come to know the Father, it is only by the transforming power of the Holy Spirit that we come to know Christ. In John 16:5–15, Jesus speaks of the work of the Holy Spirit. In verses 13–15, He says, "However, when He, the Spirit of truth has come, He will guide you into all truth; for He will not speak on His own authority, but whatever He hears He will speak…He will glorify Me, for He will take of what is Mine and declare it to you. All things that the Father has are Mine. Therefore I said that He will take of Mine and declare it to you." As Christ spoke only what He heard the Father speak and did only what He saw the Father do, so the Holy Spirit speaks and does only what Christ speaks and does. Through His empowerment in our lives, Christ continues His ministry in His people. Thus, when our minds and spirits are transformed by the Holy Spirit, we see and hear Christ and thus hear and see the Father. They are one and They speak and act as one.

Why must the Holy Spirit reveal Christ to us so Christ can reveal the Father? Because Scripture clearly tells us that in our fallen state, our natural state, that which we inherited from our father Adam (see Rom. 5), we cannot hear spiritual things, nor can we see spiritual things, nor can we understand spiritual things (see 1 Cor. 2). We are spiritually dead—and dead men and women do not see or hear and certainly cannot understand. Therefore, the Holy Spirit must enable us to see, hear, and understand Christ, and thus to see, hear, and understand the Father. How unspeakable is the grace whereby the Holy Spirit opens the eyes of our understanding and gives us wisdom and knowledge of God that we may know the riches and glory of our inheritance as His sons and daughters (see Eph. 1:17–18). All of this and more is from the Father's eternal purpose, which He accomplished in Christ and implements in our lives by the empowering presence of the Holy Spirit.

Paul tells us in Ephesians chapter 1 that the Father chose us in Christ before the foundation of the world and predestined us to adoption as sons and daughters through Jesus Christ, by the Holy Spirit, according to the good pleasure of His will. Think of it! In our natural state, whether we were born and raised in bars or in a church family, we were spiritual orphans, wandering through life subject to every kind of deception and abuse and, ultimately, to eternal death. But God, in His mercy and love, made us to be His children. We are recipients of His everlasting, unconditional love as He brings us into an intimate, abiding relationship with Christ, by the Holy Spirit, transforming us to become like Christ, thereby releasing us from eternal death and giving us eternal life.

Where our natural fathers might abandon us, our heavenly Father will never leave us or forsake us. Where our natural fathers might ignore us, our heavenly Father sees all that we do and guides and directs us in all things. Where our natural fathers have limitations and failures and faults, our heavenly Father is the sovereign God of the whole universe. He is the creator and sustainer of all things; He is the ruler of all things; He rises up and puts down nations; His will is unchanging; and what He has said He will do and what He has promised is assured. What faith, what hope, what love is stirred in us when we consider that He is our Father!

Not only can we call Him Father, but in our regeneration through Christ by the empowerment of the Holy Spirit we are spiritually born into His family and He gives us the spirit of adoption whereby we also cry out, "Abba, Father" (Rom. 8:15). As His children we cry out, "Daddy." We were without merit, without hope, and without any ability to do anything that pleases Him, subject only to eternal judgment and death. Yet He brought us into the intimate, personal relationship of being His son or daughter. It is out of that Father-child relationship that He allows us to know Him more and more, as we come to love Him more and more, as we come to abide in Christ more and more by the empowering of the Holy Spirit. It is out of that relationship that our God-given spirit cries out to Him in loving adoration as He becomes the source of our love, our hope, our joy, and our faith. As Charles Spurgeon said, "It is a sweet compound of faith that knows God to be my Father, love that loves Him as my Father, joy that rejoices in Him as my Father, fear that trembles to disobey Him because He is my Father and a confident affection and trustfulness that relies upon Him, and cast itself wholly upon Him, because it knows by the infallible witness of the Holy Spirit, that Jehovah, the God of earth and heaven, is the Father of my heart."[1]

As God's Children We Cry Out, "Daddy."

In my early years, God's Fatherhood was simply a vague concept that at the time simply meant that somewhere in some distant place was someone who I related to in some distant manner. It was only later, through the enlightenment of the Word, through the experiences and maturing process of life as I focused on Christ by the leading of the Holy Spirit, that I came into an understanding of His true Fatherhood and the relationship and responsibility and absolute joy born out of that understanding. In spite of where I started, by God's grace, His Fatherhood did not remain a vague concept but became a reality in our lives as He continued over and over to prove Himself faithful. He was our Father even when it was not apparent that we were His children, even when we did not understand His love for us, and even in those times when we may have walked away from Him for a while.

Saints, as we are His children forever, so our children are always our children, no matter what they do. If they are following God, rejoice and be glad. If they are not following God, never give up; never lose faith; never look down on them; never stop praying for them. Even if they were raised in a southern Oklahoma bar with no concept of God, do not write them off. If they are spiritually injured, lying on the side of life's road and unable to help themselves, do not be like the priest in Jesus' story of the Good Samaritan and walk by on the other side of the road, leaving them alone and hurting. We should not care how they started down that road. Our focus should be on them finishing the journey walking with their heavenly Father. Those who are God's children were chosen by Him before the beginning of time. Before He formed them in the womb, He knew them (see Isa. 44:2). Before they were born, He sanctified them and ordained them to be one of His obedient children. Never stop praying for the day when He will reveal Himself to them as their true Father.

O righteous Father! The world has not known You, but I have known You; and these have known that You sent Me. And I have declared to them Your name, and will declare it, that the love with which You loved Me may be in them, and I in them

JOHN 17:25–26

Behold what manner of love the Father has bestowed on us, that we should be called children of God!

1 JOHN 3:1A

Endnote
1. The Fatherhood of God, Sermon by C.H. Spurgeon, September 12, 1858.

Chapter Six

Learning From God's Humble Servants

God's process of bringing me from seeing the seedy side of life to seeing the glory of His grace consisted of Holy Spirit-enlightened study of God's Word, of God speaking to us through our experiences, and of Him putting people in our lives to sow seeds of His love that He then watered, nourished, cultivated, pruned, and shaped as the years went by.

Even in my early life when I did not know Him, God was faithful to give me a maternal grandmother who loved Christ, who prayed for me, who lived Him before me, and who spoke of Him with love whenever I was with her. I now realize how thankful I am that she lovingly shared Christ with me even though my life at home was so different from her way of life. I am sure that the Lord used her to plant the seeds of truth in my spirit that later grew to be fruitful vines. She was a loving grandmother, but don't get the idea that Grandma Foster coddled me into loving her. I lived with her and my grandfather for a year or so and she made sure

I understood the Lord's loving discipline as well as His loving grace and mercy. She understood that God intended for me to grow up to be a man; therefore, she did not "over mother" or "over grandmother" me. She required me to do my share of work (fitted to my age), but she also kept a dish of lemon drops on her kitchen counter that was always available to me. She readily dispensed discipline when it was needed but she also readily dispensed grandmotherly hugs and kisses when they were needed, and sometimes even when they were not, which I always appreciated. She did not hesitate to tell me that she was not happy that I had gotten married so young, but she was also quick to show her love to Joyce whenever Joyce needed it.

Grandfather Foster did not express himself the way my grandmother did, but he lived a life of care and love for others that spoke to me as loudly as words. Until his later years he always owned a small café where people came to eat his plate lunches, but especially a piece of one of his pies for dessert. Although he never finished high school, he was full of wisdom gained from the struggles of life. He taught me the value of fellowship around a table. Grandpa Foster would fix a batch of biscuits, put a can of sorghum molasses and real butter on the table, then share his wisdom with me as the two of us mixed the sorghum and butter together on our plate, spread it on a biscuit, and thoroughly enjoy every bite we took. There at the kitchen table he talked to me about the value of hard work and being very responsible with hard-earned money. I do not think that he purposed or planned out our times together; they simply grew out of who he was. I particularly enjoyed the way he usually punctuated his advice with a story. One that stands out in my memory even today was the time during the Great Depression when he and my grandmother had nothing but a sack of oranges to eat for a whole week. He never blamed anyone, he never complained, and he never expressed regrets for the tough times that he went through. He just did what he had to do.

As with most things, I have come to appreciate him more later in life as I have realized how much he expressed his love for me through his actions. One of the most vivid examples of this was the last time I saw him alive. We were in Vernon on one of our regular trips to visit family, and Mother told me that he was at work but wanted me to come by to see him. He was no longer able to run a café, but he still worked as a night watchman. When I got there he gave me a pie that he had baked just for me. It was my favorite pie and I knew how much love he had put into baking it. Looking back, that pie was as precious to me as the water that David's men brought to him from the well of Bethlehem. David was spiritual enough to recognize that the sacrifice of his men made the water far too precious to drink, so he poured it out to the Lord. I wish that I had recognized then just how precious that act of sacrificial love was that my grandfather expressed to me that day, but, alas, I did not. I thanked him and gave him a big hug, but that was so inadequate. I did think of him, however, each time I savored a bite of that pie. To this day I have never forgotten his example of how much a small and seemingly insignificant expression of love can impact the person to whom it is given.

Grandmother Foster also gave me my first vivid example of a faithful servant who had nothing to give but gave everything she had and everything she was to the Lord. She never learned to drive a car, so she walked to church for every service until she could no longer climb the 20 or so steps up to the front door of the sanctuary. And even when she could no longer go to church services, her Bible was a constant companion as the Lord comforted her through His Word. She also exemplified the fulfillment of one of the greatest "ministries" to which any woman can be called: praying for her children, her grandchildren, and her great-grandchildren.

She was an early example that God put in my life of those who "silently serve." (Oh, the blessedness of serving or giving when no one but God knows.) They are the ones who will never speak great glowing words that tickle our intellect or stir our emotions, but will proclaim Jesus Christ with a thankful heart to those whom He places in their path. They will never write books to be put on library shelves and admired from afar, but are those who, by their lifetime of faithful service, write volumes of God's love upon our hearts. They will never do great exploits to be seen by others, but, unknown to others, will move mountains by their unceasing prayers. They are those who know that obedience to God is what matters and who, while never proclaiming their good deeds, serve God with all of their heart and mind and soul and spirit. Some, like Simeon and Anna, will see the longing of their heart fulfilled (see Luke 2). But most will be counted among the unnumbered multitude who will never know in this lifetime how many people were blessed by their prayers and faithful service. They are those who faithfully serve God where they are, with what they have, in the best way they know how.

The prime example of such service that God has kept before me these past 53 years of marriage is my wife Joyce. She has always served others who needed her help with a rare balance of loving care and the ability to cut through protocol and do what was best for the other person or what was right under whatever circumstances she was facing. Her gift of serving was one of her reasons for becoming a nurse and for deciding to stay at home to care for her children. Joyce's heart has always been to be there to serve family and friends and church wherever she could.

The Prime Example of Service that God has Kept Before Me These Past 53 Years is My Wife Joyce.

As is pleasing to the Lord, when it came time to care for her mother, Joyce was there. Joyce's mother was diabetic, and even though Joyce continually worked with her, she eventually lost both her legs to the disease. When the surgeon informed Joyce that her mother's second leg would have to be amputated, he told her that because of her weak heart, her mother would probably not make it through the operation and, even if she did, would probably live only a few months. Joyce's mother did make it through the operation, but when we brought her home to live with us she was down to about 90 pounds and so weak that it looked as though the doctor might have been right in his estimate of her remaining time. However, as Joyce is so gifted to do, through prayer-filled diligent, determined, loving care, Joyce nursed her mother back to health.

Because her mother had lost both legs, Joyce had to lift her out of bed in the morning and into her wheelchair, then out of and back into her wheelchair about 20 times a day, and finally, out of her wheelchair and back into bed at night. At first, Joyce managed this well, but as her mother grew healthier and gained weight it became harder and harder for Joyce to lift her. After a year of Joyce's mother getting stronger and Joyce's back getting weaker, we had to make the difficult decision to move her mother to a nursing home for care. It was an extremely difficult decision, but it was the best thing for both Joyce and her mother.

After the move was made, Joyce focused on making sure that her mother received all the care she needed. For the remaining five years of her mother's life, Joyce continued to be there for her. In addition to caring for her mother, Joyce was also the "responsible party" for my Down's syndrome sister for the last ten years of my sister's life, and has been the "responsible party" for one of her aunts and a retarded cousin for the past ten years or so. In all of these cases Joyce became very well-known to the doctors, nurses, and administrative staff, who knew that she would be sure to let them know when something needed to change.

To her friends, Joyce has been an example of Scripture's call for us to lay down our lives for our spiritual brothers and sisters. When her friend Linda was hurt and could not take care of her house and family, Joyce and Cindy went to help clean Linda's house and to do whatever else needed to be done. While she and Cindy were there working away, the phone rang. Since Linda could not get out of bed, Joyce answered the phone. "Hello, this is Joyce."

The lady who called responded with surprise, "Joyce Graham?"

"Yes," Joyce replied. "Linda fell and hurt herself, and Cindy and I are here helping her."

"But why are you there?" the lady asked. "You are not part of our home group."

Joyce just shook her head. "Linda is my friend, she needs help, and I am here to help her."

I am not sure the lady ever completely understood, but once again Joyce had cut through a mental silo to do what was right. Linda understood and was very appreciative. However, much of Joyce's service to friends, family, and church has gone unnoticed and, in some cases, unappreciated, but she has always done it "as unto the Lord," which is the kind of loving service that pleases Him.

Charles Spurgeon was called the "prince of preachers" and the "people's preacher." It is said that he personally preached to over ten million people during his relatively short life. No one knows how many people have been influenced by listening to him, by reading his published sermons, books, and other writings, or through the ministries that he established. But do we remember today the country preacher in the small church where Spurgeon, at the age of 16, was changed forever as the preacher delivered his message from Isaiah and, in obedience to the Holy Spirit's leading, challenged Spurgeon to simply look to the Lord for his salvation? What can we say was the eternal impact of that country preacher who was faithful to serve God where he was with what he had been given to work with and was obedient to minister to a young boy who would eventually influence millions of people? And how can we measure the influence of Spurgeon's grandfather who allowed Spurgeon to spend hours in his library reading Christian books?

We usually give the apostles their rightful honor, but how often do we consider the converted believers who faithfully shared their newfound faith and saw the Church grow daily? Or do we remember or even know of those throughout the history of the Church who faithfully met together in homes to pray and then marveled as the Holy Spirit brought true revival that resulted in multitudes being saved and churches filled to overflowing with men and women who were on fire for God, replacing those dying embers that had grown cold through religious formalism? Do we remember those two or three or four who prayed together and saw the Irish, Welsh, European, and American revivals of the 1800s and early 1900s? And if we do know of them or remember them at all, do we thank God for their faithfulness to pray and then follow their example?

In contrast, in the celebrity cult that seems to so dominate our secular culture and, unfortunately, our religious culture, only those who achieve elevated outward status are considered worthy of honor and praise. They are given a priority position in the use of our time, our energy, and our money, and thereby they are given God-like status in our lives even though they usually give little or nothing in return for our praise and adoration except to tickle our ears with what we want to hear. But Paul prayed that all of us would come to understand the love of Christ and proclaimed that we were all one in Christ and all sons and daughters of God in Christ. Scripture tells us that all of His children should be priests and kings unto God. Jesus said in Mark 12:42–43 that the poor widow who gave "two very small copper coins, worth only a fraction of a penny" (NIV) out of her heart of thankfulness had given more than all those who gave out of their abundance rather than from their heart. The poor widow gave all that she had in her offering to God with an understanding that all things are His and she gave in responsive, loving obedience. On the other hand, the rich gave what they could spare out of what they believed to be theirs. Thus, according to Jesus, the poor widow gave more than all the rest.

We give temporary honor to outward appearances, but God gives eternal honor to those of humble spirit. All of His humble servants are due our respect and gratitude and thankfulness for their dedication to the Lord as they daily and sacrificially and obediently serve. Near the end of the Sermon on the Mount, Jesus said, "Many will say to Me in that day, 'Lord, Lord, have we not prophesied in Your name, cast out demons in Your name, and done many wonders in Your name?' And then I will declare to them, 'I never knew you; depart from Me, you who practice lawlessness!'" (Matt. 7:22–23). Jesus said that they must depart from Him because they did not do those things in humble obedience to Him. But He knows and will embrace those who have humbly served Him wherever He has placed them doing whatever He has given them to do. They are ordinary people living ordinary lives in extraordinary faith and love in Christ, by the power of the Holy Spirit.

We Give Temporary Honor to Outward Appearances, but God Gives Eternal Honor to Those of Humble Spirit.

Over the years I have come to see that the true measure of men or women is not the monuments that they build to themselves, or the titles they give to themselves, or the books that they may write, or even the sermons that they might preach. For as Thomas à Kempis said in Chapter III of *The Imitation of Christ*:

> Tell me, where are all those masters and teachers, whom you knew so well, while they were with you, and flourished in their learning? Their places in the church are now filled by others, who perhaps never

have one thought concerning them. While they lived they seemed to be so important, but now no one even speaks of them. Oh how quickly the glory of the world passes away! It would have been better if their life had agreed with their knowledge. For then all of their reading and study would have been for a good and eternal purpose. For how many perish through empty learning as they care little for serving God. And because they love to be great rather than to be humble, they therefore become vain in their imaginations. He only is truly great who has great love for others. He is truly great who considers himself as nothing and considers all things as nothing that he might win Christ. And he is truly a man of wisdom who does the will of God and forsakes his own will.[1]

This was written in the 1400s, but see how true it is even today. How much we see the former and how little we see the latter, yet how much we give our honor to the former while God gives His honor to the latter. How often we see those who desire to sit at the head of the table seeking men's honor and how much we need to see those who sit first at the foot of the table but are then called by God to come up and sit by Him and partake of His glory. How often do we see men and women who flaunt their academic degrees and look down with disdain upon those who have not achieved to their assumed status? But how much more should we look to those who have been trained in Christ's school of humility, knowing that without Christ they can do nothing, and who therefore honor all of God's children regardless of their status in life?

Isaiah 57:15 says, "For thus says the High and Lofty One who inhabits eternity, whose name is Holy: 'I dwell in the high and holy place, with him who has a contrite and humble spirit, to revive the spirit of the humble, and to revive the heart of the contrite ones.'" We look to outward appearances, but God looks at the heart. He who is creator of all things, He who gives life and breath to all things, He who holds the universe in

His hand, lifts up those who have a contrite and humble spirit to sit with Him in high and holy places. How thankful I am that God has allowed me from the beginning of my walk with Him to know men and women who could, but who would not, proclaim with Paul, "I have been crucified with Christ; it is no longer I who live, but Christ who lives in me; and the life which I now live in the flesh I live by faith in the Son of God, who loved me and gave Himself for me" (Gal. 2:20).

In Christ we have the perfect example of the attitude we should have. He is God, the One through whom and for whom all things were created, the One into whose hands all authority has been given, the One who is above all things in heaven and earth, yet He humbled Himself to the point of death on the cross, becoming cursed and taking on the sins of the world even though He could have called down legions of angels to defend Himself. He who was from the beginning, He who is one with the Father, He who was clothed with the glory of the Godhead before there was a world, humbled Himself to pay the price for our sins and reconcile us to the Father. We make much of His physical suffering, but to me the utmost suffering was the spiritual suffering that He endured in obedience to the Father. The spiritual pain and anguish Jesus experienced at that moment of being forsaken is more than we can possibly comprehend. Yet Scripture tells us that we should have the mind of Christ. But in spite of Christ's example and in spite of Scripture's warnings that God resists the proud but gives grace to the humble, so many of those who should be examples of Christ's humility in obedient service to God strive to put themselves first, promoting their own agenda and striving to be known above others rather than, like Christ, laying their lives down for the brethren.

So many are like those who walk along the beach, always looking back at their footprints to make sure others know where they have walked. But time and tides come and wash away their footprints and no one knows that they were even there. Others also leave footprints, but stop to build sandcastles, thinking that others will see what they have built and marvel at their ability to build such a fine castle. But time and tides come and wash away all that they have built and no one knows that they were even there. There are others who even bring wood and bricks, thinking that they will build something that will stand forever and many generations will know how great they were to build such a structure. But time and tides come and wash away any trace of what they built and no one knows that they were even there. But there are a few who walk on the beach never looking back but only looking up to their Lord for direction. They care nothing that anyone else knows where they have walked or what they have done or if they will be remembered at all. They care only that they are obedient to their Lord and please Him in all that they do. And time and tides come but they cannot wash away what these have done because their service to the Lord is written upon His heart and it can never be taken away.

> *For you see your calling, brethren, that not many wise according to the flesh, not many mighty, not many noble, are called. But God has chosen the foolish things of the world to put to shame the wise, and God has chosen the weak things of the world to put to shame the things which are mighty; and the base things of the world and the things which are despised God has chosen, and the things which are not, to bring to nothing the things that are, that no flesh should glory in His presence. But of Him you are in Christ Jesus, who became for us wisdom from God—and righteousness and sanctification and redemption—that, as it is written, "He who glories, let him glory in the Lord"*
>
> 1 CORINTHIANS 1:26–31

> *Let this mind be in you which was also in Christ Jesus, who, being in the form of God, did not consider it robbery to be equal with*

God, but made Himself of no reputation, taking the form of a bondservant, and coming in the likeness of men. And being found in appearance as a man, He humbled Himself and became obedient to the point of death, even the death of the cross

PHILIPPIANS 2:5–8

Endnote
1. Thomas à Kempis, The Imitation of Christ (Uhrichsville, Ohio: Barbour Publishing, Inc., 1984).

Chapter Seven

Early Training: Whatever It Takes

Joyce and I married the November after I graduated from high school. She was "nearly 16" and I was "nearly 18." Our first child, Michael, was born 11 months later. (Joyce got a rose at the Mother's Day service for being the youngest mother in attendance.) When you start in the bottom of a ditch with no ladder, it is a task just to get to level ground, but through 53 years of marriage, four children, nine grandchildren, and four great-grandchildren, we can testify with no hesitation that God has always been faithful to care for us. Even in those early years when we did not have much common sense, as our decision to get married so young and having only 25 cents to our name when we got back from getting married clearly indicate, God nevertheless was faithful to provide what we needed. He also gave us a desire to continue the process, doing whatever it took to press through and overcome whatever circumstances we encountered.

Many people were convinced that we had ruined our lives by getting married so young and had therefore condemned us to a life of misery and despair, of always struggling just to make ends meet. Some were even bold enough to tell us directly. One of my high school coaches called Joyce out of class and told her in no uncertain terms that she had ruined my life…and he was one of the nicer ones. No one gave us much hope for anything. And, realistically, it was like we were starting to run a race, only to voluntarily throw a 50-pound weight over each shoulder just as the starting gun went off. It wasn't smart; it did put us behind; but at least we got in the race. And thank God we did not know when we started that it was going to be an uphill steeplechase rather than a short sprint.

I am also thankful that we did not know any better than to take full responsibility for our lives and to follow the path that we thought would improve our lot in life. Since we were so young and had not yet learned how to hear God totally and follow His directions, we spent our early marriage and college years mostly doing what we thought we needed to do. Although we went to church and prayed and trusted God to the extent we knew how to trust Him, for the most part our efforts were directed toward surviving the immediate while working toward a better future. We lived as best we could, but, not even knowing that there was a Holy Spirit who could guide and comfort us, we did not know how to fully walk in His loving care and guidance. As a consequence, we made many mistakes and several times we had to stop, back up, and get on the right road again. As one of my high school teachers put it, we had several flat tires that had to be fixed before we could continue on our journey. But looking back we can now see that in spite of our ignorance, in spite of how young we were spiritually and physically, God was directing our lives and preparing us for the future.

During the first year of our marriage I worked at several jobs making just enough money to get by and thinking that it would probably be what

I would do the rest of my life. I could not see that there was any way I could go to college, and even if I did, I thought I probably didn't have the ability to make it through the classes. Then, through a friend, I got to try out and received a football scholarship at Cameron Jr. College (now Cameron University) in Lawton, Oklahoma. The scholarship provided me with tuition, an apartment in "vet village," and $30 a month to live on.

Vet village was a group of army barracks that had been divided into "bare necessity" apartments that had inside Sheetrock™ on one side of the apartment and just the studs and the backside of the next apartment's Sheetrock™ on the other side. We were thankful to have a place to live, but with only one layer dividing each apartment, we had to learn to talk as quietly as we could and to not listen to our next-door neighbors. We also had to learn how to live on what we had. We found a local dairy where we could get a gallon of whole milk for 50 cents as long as we brought our own glass jug to fill. We would skim the cream off the top and make butter by putting the cream in a jar and shaking it for a long time. Sometimes we made whipped cream. (Unfortunately, red beans and whipped cream did not make for a very good diet.)

Between school, practice, games, and study, I found odd jobs on weekends and worked full-time over the Christmas holidays. In addition, we picked up soft drink bottles on the roadside that we could redeem for 3 cents a bottle. I also did some work for a relative who owned a gas station and for a second cousin who owned an upholstery shop and a used furniture and appliance store. He let us buy a washing machine for $35 and pay it out at $5 a month.

Joyce made some extra money by washing diapers for 25 cents a load for other mothers in the village who had babies. She would wash them and the mothers would come by later to pick them up. One time she washed several loads of Mike's diapers and hung them on the clothesline to dry. It was freezing cold that day, with a howling wind, and those diapers froze in a horizontal position on the clothesline before she could get back inside. As I said, we did whatever it took to get by.

We Did Whatever It Took to Get By.

One day Joyce took Mike and walked to the little store near the campus and bought a dozen eggs, some milk, and some bread. When she broke open the first egg the next morning, she was surprised to see that it had a double yolk. Over the next several days she was amazed to discover that every egg in the carton was a double-yolk egg. Considering how tight our food budget was, she went back to the store, walked up to the checkout counter, and told the clerk that the dozen eggs that she had bought on her last visit all had double yolks. She asked him where the double yolk eggs were so she could buy some more of them. At first the clerk did not understand what she was asking. Joyce explained again that all 12 eggs had double yolks and she wanted some more just like that. He then told her that eggs normally had just one yolk and that it was very unusual for even one egg to have a double yolk, much less a whole dozen. Joyce decided that it must have been a special blessing and she reluctantly bought a dozen "regular" eggs. Oh, did I say that we were a little naive in those days?

With all that we had to deal with, it only took one semester for me to understand that I was not going to make it playing football. As the old saying goes, "I was small but I was slow," and grit and determination without talent will not take you very far. However, that semester did show me that I could study and make good grades, which gave me hope that if I worked hard enough I could finish college. Joyce and I took Mike and went back to Vernon to work for the summer and then headed to Lubbock to figure out how we could get by while I went to Texas Tech.

In Lubbock I registered for classes, got a job washing dairy trucks at night, and found a little house near the campus and the dairy. The location of the house allowed me to walk both to class and to work, so we only drove the car when we had to. It seemed to be the perfect setup. However, when we moved into the house and the first west Texas sandstorm blew in, Joyce discovered that if she looked under the window sills she could see straight through to the outside. Convinced that our son would freeze if we stayed there through the winter, Joyce started looking for another place to live. About the time that she found a much better place for us I got a job on a freight dock making union wages. The freight dock job was a real blessing because it allowed me to support my family and still go to school. I could be at school from 8:00 to 12:00 in the morning and then work on the dock from 1:00 to 9:00 at night. In those days I did not need much sleep, so I would come home from the dock, get cleaned up, and study until midnight or so. Then I was up the next morning at 4:00 to start the routine all over again.

After we had gotten settled down somewhat, Joyce began nursing school, which was something she had always wanted to do. She was not quite sure that she could do all that would be required, but she was determined to do her best and see what happened. She loved nursing school and gave herself wholeheartedly to her studies and training. During this time she became pregnant with our daughter Cindy. She was about three months along when we took Mike and traveled to Austin for her state board exam so she could get her license. Even after studying for the exam, Joyce was still not sure that she could pass the test, so we were both ecstatic when she got the results: She had scored one of the highest grades in her class. It is amazing what can happen if you pray without ceasing and purposely prepare for what is ahead.

After graduating from nursing school and getting her license, Joyce began working full-time in the hospital where she had trained. She was assigned to the obstetrics floor. One day when she was about six months along and definitely showing, she was helping a husband and wife who had arrived for the birth of their fourth child. They had three daughters and really wanted this one to be a boy. After they were assigned a room and Joyce had helped the wife get into bed, the lady went into final contractions. Joyce immediately went to the head nurse, told her what was happening, and watched in utter shock as the head nurse ran to find a doctor. Joyce never did understand why she did not use the phone that was right there at the nurses' station. Knowing that the lady would need help, Joyce ran back into the room just in time to deliver the child. She was holding the baby in her hands when their doctor came into the room. Joyce handed him the baby. The doctor told her to get an umbilical cord kit. She got the kit and accidentally spilled disinfectant fluid all over his expensive suit, but then she helped him cut the newborn's umbilical cord. Realizing that Joyce was six months pregnant, the doctor told her to sit down before she passed out or had her own child prematurely.

After resting for a few minutes, Joyce went outside and told the father that his child had been born and was doing fine.

"Is it a boy or a girl?" the father eagerly asked.

Joyce realized that she could not remember, but then said, "I think it is a boy."

The father was so excited to learn that he now had a son. When Joyce went back into the room, however, she discovered that the baby was a girl and not a boy. Chagrined, she went up to the doctor. "I told the father the baby was a boy."

"Well," the doctor said, somewhat amused, "since you are the one who made the mistake, you have to be the one to go out and tell the father."

Joyce looked at the doctor for a moment and then said, "Okay, I will.

But since I delivered the baby and you didn't, I don't think you should charge them for it." She left the room, walked up to the father, and said, "I am so sorry. I told you that the baby was a boy, but it was a girl."

He paused a minute, taking in this new bit of news. Then he hugged Joyce and graciously told her, "That's all right, hon. I know you were upset, and at least I thought I had a son for ten minutes or so."

Later Joyce found out that the doctor, in fact, did not charge them a delivery fee.

By the time Cindy was ready to be born, Joyce had been sent home twice by the doctor after going in thinking she was ready to deliver. The second time, the doctor told her that it was still two weeks until her due date and that she was not to come back until she was actually ready to deliver. With this admonition in mind, Joyce nearly waited too long. Only a few days later, the same doctor who had sent Joyce home for two weeks had to rush to the hospital to deliver Cindy. When Joyce arrived in the delivery room, she wasn't dilating enough and she couldn't get Cindy to move. She heard the nurse tell the doctor that her blood pressure had "skyrocketed." They gave her something to relax her and she began to feel like she was floating in the air. At the same time she was very concerned that the delivery would go well and that the baby would be all right. Suddenly, she had a vision of God holding the earth in His hand. He was so large that she was taken aback by the sight of Him and she could not say anything. Then she heard God say, "I hold the world in My hand. Do not worry. You and your baby will be fine." She felt her body relax in time to hear the doctor say that the baby was a girl. In those days before ultrasound, we did not know whether the child would be a boy or a girl until it was delivered. After Joyce knew that it was a girl, she fell asleep and did not wake up until she was back in her room.

"I Hold the World In My Hand. Do Not Worry."

When she woke up, she asked three different nurses to bring Cindy to her, but no one did. Because of the way the nurses acted, Joyce began to worry about Cindy. She got out of bed and started down the hall to see her. A nurse grabbed her by the arm.

"You need to go back to your room. Your baby is being cleaned up."

That did not satisfy Joyce. "I have worked on OB, and I know it does not take this long to clean up a baby. I want to see my baby right now. If there is anything wrong with her, I want to know about it."

"Joyce, calm down," the nurse told her. "Go back to your room and I will send the head nurse to talk to you."

As Joyce returned to her room, she felt sick all over and started to think the worst. She began to cry and called out to God, "Please let my daughter live!" Then she remembered the vision that she had in the delivery room and began to feel a little better. Still, she could not completely shake her worries.

A few minutes later, the head nurse came in. "Your daughter has a purple burn and bumpy skin over one side of her face," she said.

A flood of relief washed over Joyce. It was not as bad as she feared. "I don't care about the burn," she said. "I just want to see Cindy."

They later told us that Cindy's stomach acid had caused the burn and that it would eventually clear up. I had seen the burn on Cindy's face myself just after she was born as they rushed by where I was standing outside the delivery room holding Mike, on their way to clean her up. It was a huge relief to find out what had caused it.

But there were other problems. "Cindy's umbilical cord had a knot in it that almost cut off her blood supply," the doctor told us. "If she had gone full-term she might have been stillborn or else born with severe physical problems. The fact that she was born two weeks early kept her from some severe problems, but the reduction in her blood flow may have caused other problems. There are several things we are concerned about, particularly the possibility that she may have an intestinal blockage. She is not keeping food down and if she does not have a bowel movement soon, we will have to do surgery to see what is wrong."

Upon receiving this news, Joyce and I spent three days worrying about Cindy and intently praying for her. On the very morning that she was scheduled for surgery, she had a bowel movement and the scheduled surgery was canceled. God had His hand on Cindy even before she was born.

After we brought Cindy home and Joyce had recovered, our daily routine consisted in leaving home in the morning in time for Joyce to drop Mike and Cindy at the sitter, drop me off at school where I would attend classes or study from 8 to 12, and then drive to the doctor's office where she worked. At lunch time Joyce would pick me up at school, take me to the freight dock, and go back to work at the doctor's office. She would then pick me up at 9:00 p.m. or later and we would go home, where I would eat, get cleaned up, and study till midnight or so.

We had a lot going on and there came a point when I began to think that it was just not worth all the effort. I was making union wages; we had two children; I was tired; so why not just stop trying? Instead of finishing school, I could just work on the freight dock or drive a truck. I found the thought quite tempting. Then one day I was loading a truck with a co-worker who was 60 years old. I appreciated how hard he worked and what a good employee he was, but as I looked at him a voice inside asked, "Is that what you want to be doing when you are 60 years old?" My answer was an immediate "NO!"

Please understand that I am in no way, shape, or form trying to say that those who do such jobs are any less than those who do not. Our worth is not measured by the job that we have. But continuing to stay where I was and continuing to do the things that I was doing was not what the Lord wanted for me. Several years before this He had given me a vision for a different future and now He was reminding me of that future. From that moment on I dedicated myself to doing whatever it took to finish school. Eventually I did finish school and we moved to Fort Worth so I could take the accounting job I had been offered with one of the "big eight" international accounting firms. (The firm was not one of the current "final four.")

From that Moment On I Dedicated Myself to Doing Whatever It Took to Finish School.

At the beginning of this chapter I said that we could look back and see that God's hand was on us to teach us and train us for what was ahead. What was ahead was a need to know how to persevere spiritually just as He had trained us to persevere in the natural. I am not talking about the old American idea that if you just try hard enough you can overcome anything. Nor am I talking about taking pride in a self-determined path of accomplishments that succeeds in the face of adversity. If our efforts for success are not part of our walk with God, they may be noteworthy but they are chasing after the wind and result in no true reward. What I am talking about is a God-given attitude that lives in the reality of the present but focuses on the reality of God and, out of our relationship with Him, looks forward to what He has for us in the future. Did Joyce and I have a clear understanding of this concept while we were going through these early years of learning to persevere in the things that we did? No, we did not. But even while we were living in the shadows of understanding of what it means to follow God, He was actively guiding us and teaching us as preparation for the future.

A parent does not expect a two-year-old child to be able to follow a map to the next room in the house, much less to the next city or next state. Naturally that child has to be raised up to the point in life of understanding what it means to go on a journey, the preparations that are necessary, the things that must be taken along, and the directions that must be followed in order to reach the destination. Spiritually, we must grow in our understanding of the same things. Just as it takes time to grow up, learning from the difficulties that we face and the triumphs that we have as preparation for adulthood, so it takes time to grow spiritually, learning from the difficulties and failures and successes that we encounter to grow into spiritual maturity. God, our loving Father, through Christ and by the Holy Spirit, teaches us, guides us, and directs us in this growth process. His purpose is to prepare us for the greater difficulties, failures, and life-changing experiences that we will face in the future as we come to know Christ more and more and grow to be more and more like Him. As our loving Father, He allows us to face difficulties and successes that require us to take responsibility and learn to trust Him as He leads, guides, and teaches us to overcome those difficulties and to see through the successes by our faith in Him and Him alone.

Too many times I have seen parents who, out of a misunderstanding of their parental responsibilities, or out of a lack of understanding of true love for their children, or out of guilt for their lack of real involvement in their children's lives, try their best to protect their children from any and every difficulty. Unfortunately, this approach usually backfires. Rather than being best for their children, it actually results in adult children who are not prepared for the difficulties they will face in the real world. It produces adult children (not adults) who are unable to take responsibility for their own actions because they have been trained to blame someone else for any failure, or even any appearance of failure, that comes their way. Ironically, these children who have been given so much usually wind up blaming their parents for their own lack of personal responsibility.

When Peter began to tell Christ how wrong He was in telling the disciples that He would be rejected by the religious leaders, would be killed, and then would rise again, Jesus looked at the disciples and rebuked Peter, saying, "Get behind Me, Satan! For you are not mindful of the things of God, but the things of men" (Mark 8:33). And just think, Jesus rebuked Peter right in front of all the other disciples. Before Jesus was crucified, Peter denied Him three times. In John chapter 21, John tells us that after His resurrection, Jesus lovingly restored Peter and then told him "by what death he would glorify God." Then He told Peter, "Follow Me." When Peter heard all of this, he turned around, looked at John, and asked Jesus, "But Lord, what about this man?" Most of us would have thought that Jesus would have put His arm around Peter's shoulder and given Peter a very consoling answer. But, in essence, Jesus told Peter, "What is that to you? Don't worry about John. You just follow Me." A bit harsh, you say? No. Jesus only spoke what He heard the Father speak and the Father knew what was best for Peter in preparing him for the future. Even though it was not what Peter wanted to hear, it was what Peter needed to hear. Out of His love for us, the Father always does what is best for us.

Our loving Father will prepare us for the future even when we do not know that He is doing so. He chose us before the beginning of time and His hand is ever on us. He guides us and teaches us in the natural and brings us into the process of transformation in which we are being prepared for our service to Him. No matter where we were in the natural, He will transform us and mold us and make us into what we are to become in Him.

The apostle John was the younger of the two "Sons of Thunder." That title tells me that he was probably ready to call down fire from heaven to vanquish all who opposed what he thought should be done. But by God's grace he became the apostle who most vividly expressed God's love. Peter cowered in fear and cursed in protest when a young girl pointed him out as a follower of Christ. But by God's grace he became a man who proclaimed Christ and in faith gave his life that Christ might be glorified. Paul was a Pharisee of Pharisees who before his encounter with Christ persecuted the Church. He was "breathing threats and murder against the disciples of the Lord" (Acts 9:1) and later testified that "many of the saints I shut up in prison…and when they were put to death, I cast my vote against them" (Acts 26:10). But by the grace of God the knowledge and zeal that he applied to persecuting the Church before Christ arrested him, he applied to becoming the foremost spokesman for Christ as Christ became the center of all that he did.

Likewise, there are many others, named and unnamed, whom God chose and trained and guided and prepared for their future service to Him. They are those who understood that the greater the problem that they encountered and overcame in service to Him, the greater was the glory to God for giving them the victory.

But as it is written, "Eye has not seen, nor ear heard, nor have entered into the heart of man the things which God has prepared for those who love Him"

1 CORINTHIANS 2:9

And not only that, but we also glory in tribulations, knowing that tribulation produces perseverance; and perseverance, character; and character, hope. Now hope does not disappoint, because the love of God has been poured out in our hearts by the Holy Spirit who was given to us

ROMANS 5:3–5

Chapter Eight

The Next Step

Joyce and I felt an excited anticipation as well as confident hope for the future as we packed up our household and moved from Lubbock to Fort Worth. We had worked hard, overcome numerous difficulties, and persevered to the end, finally completing college. I was now ready to focus on doing whatever it took to become an excellent employee of the international public accounting firm that had hired me. Both of us looked forward to becoming part of a Fort Worth church and raising Mike and Cindy with many of the benefits that we did not have when we were growing up. As far as we knew at the time, this would be the pattern of our lives for many years.

We arrived in Fort Worth and were settled in our apartment a few days before I was to report for work. I called the firm's office, talked to the partner who had recruited me, and let him know that we had moved in and I was ready to go to work. To my surprise he told me that I could start the next morning. I was very excited about my new job and could hardly wait to begin, so I told him that I would be there. On Thursday morning I arrived at the office, spent two hours filling out forms, and was then sent to a client's office to help a tax senior on a large oil and gas job. By noon on Saturday I had 30 hours to put on my first time report. This became the regular pattern of my work for the rest of the time that I was with the firm. Such "above and beyond" effort was just the nature of a job where providing quality service to clients was the primary focus around which everything else in life had to revolve. In those days, "quality of life" was not a concept of employment in an international public accounting firm and particularly not in the firm that I worked for. The nine years I spent with the firm, with its "no mistakes allowed" atmosphere, were very demanding and very challenging, but they were also very rewarding. I loved to serve clients and there was a great deal of satisfaction in knowing that we had provided our clients with the highest quality service possible.

After our move to Fort Worth, God blessed us with the opportunity to serve in a loving, mainline denominational church of the same denomination which we had been married in, had dedicated Mike and Cindy in, and had faithfully attended for many years. We quickly became involved in many church activities, including teaching classes and serving on various committees. I became the church lay leader and helped the "earn every merit badge the old-fashioned way" scoutmaster of the troop that was sponsored by the church and in which Mike became an Eagle Scout. Joyce helped in the children's department and in many other activities where she could. Today we still have many fond memories of the good times we had and the many friends we made during those years. But let me tell you about the most vivid example from our denominational years of God teaching us that we were to turn to Him, pray in faith, and wait to see Him extraordinarily go beyond our understanding of normal church life.

After a few years of being actively involved in the Fort Worth church, Joyce and I were trying to decide whether or not to have another child. After I graduated from college, Joyce decided to be a full-time mother and homemaker. Mike was 11 and Cindy was 7 and we could have been very happy raising only two children. However, God gave both of us a desire to have another child to love. We went to our pastor to discuss it with him and he advised us to pray about it and see what God would do. We prayed about it, felt like we heard from God, and made the decision to have one more child. Sure enough, Joyce became pregnant during the first month that we started praying. Although at the time we only knew the Holy Spirit by name, we now know that He not only led us to our decision but also prompted me to pray that God would bless us with twins. To build our faith, the Holy Spirit prompted me to pray for what He had already done and thus to teach us that when we pray in accordance with His will, what we ask will be (see 1 John 5:14–15). I found out later that when Joyce was about 12 she wrote in her "little book" that she wanted to get married and have twins. I think she had forgotten about it by the time we got married and with two children already, the thought of twins was at the very back of her mind.

The Thought of Twins was at the Very Back of Her Mind.

Joyce is only 5'2" tall, and late in the pregnancy it looked as though the baby she was carrying started just under her neck and went all the way down to her knees. At least, that's the way she said it felt to her. During the latter part of her pregnancy, she usually wore a green flowing maternity dress that she dubbed "the tent." That was her name for it, not mine. To drive her car she had to push the seat back, lean back as far as she could, and stretch to reach the pedals. One day she was hurrying down the road when she heard a siren behind her. She looked in the rearview mirror, saw the policeman, and pulled over to the side of the road to wait for him. The policemen walked up to the car, did a double take when he looked at Joyce, and asked, "Are you on your way to the hospital?"

"No," Joyce replied, "I am on my way to see a friend."

The officer continued to look at her stomach rather than directly at her and said, "Well, this time I will just give you a verbal warning, but try to slow down." He then folded his ticket book and almost ran back to his car. I guess he just did not have the heart to give a ticket to a woman in her condition and he sure did not want to be the one to help deliver her baby.

About a week before she delivered, Joyce went in for her scheduled doctor's visit. Her doctor also stared at her stomach and promptly scolded her for getting so big. Joyce told him that she thought she was going to have twins because one baby could not possibly kick and push in every direction at once, which was what she was experiencing. However, after the doctor examined her and heard only one heartbeat, he declared that she was going to have an eight-pound girl.

One week later, and six weeks before her scheduled delivery date, Joyce's water broke in the middle of the night. She woke me up and we quickly called a friend from church who had already offered to stay with Mike and Cindy when Joyce had to go to the hospital. After she arrived, Joyce and I got in the car and rushed to the hospital. For the next several hours Joyce experienced severe contractions with excruciating pain in her back while the nurse who periodically checked on her kept saying that she had not dilated enough. My feeble attempts to help her did nothing for her and my attempt to rub her back served only to elicit a response of, "Don't touch me!" But the next time the nurse checked Joyce, things had suddenly changed and it became a mad rush to get her to the delivery room. I was sent to the father's waiting room and told that I should watch the delivery lights. If the pink light came on, it was a girl. If the blue light came on, it was a boy. Today that seems so quaint, antiquated, old-fashioned, and funny, doesn't it?

Just after I got seated in the waiting room, a man a little younger than me came in, accompanied by his father. I introduced myself to them both and started a conversation with the father. The son did not want to talk. The father told me that they were waiting for his daughter-in-law to deliver their fourth child. His son already had four daughters by his first wife and three daughters by his current wife. They just knew that this one was going to be a boy.

We continued our conversation until I saw the blue light come on. I ran out to the hall where a nurse met me.

"Mr. Graham, you have twin sons," she said excitedly.

I know that my jaw must have dropped because the nurse stayed with me for a few minutes to make sure I did not faint or something.

"Can I see them—and Joyce?" I asked.

"Not right now," the nurse replied. "It will be a little while yet before you can go back."

While I was waiting, all I could think about was how God had blessed us with the twin sons He had prompted me to pray for. On my way to call family and everyone else I could think of, I kept singing, "Praise God from whom all blessings flow…."

Joyce later told me that they did indeed have to hurry her into the delivery room. The doctor and nurses were expecting only one baby, and when Brad was born Joyce heard the nurse say, "It's a boy." But then Joyce heard the nurse scream, "Doctor, there's another one. We have twins." Joyce's regular doctor was out of town and another doctor had to do the delivery. When her regular doctor got back from vacation he was very surprised to learn that rather than having an eight-pound girl as he had predicted, Joyce had delivered two four-pound boys.

Later that day, as I was walking down the first floor hall of the hospital with Mike and Cindy, I saw the man with whom I had talked in the waiting room that morning walking toward me. He was shaking his head from side to side and as he came up to me he looked at me and said, "It's just not fair. It's just not fair. We had another girl and you had two sons." He kept right on walking. Remember, this was his eighth granddaughter. I am sure that he loved her very much, but he really had his heart set on having a grandson.

Because they were premature and so small, Brad and Matt had to stay in the hospital until they had gained enough weight and were strong enough to go home. Going home without her babies was not a good thing for Joyce. She was a terrific mother who loved her children and loved being a mother. But on top of having to deal with leaving Brad and Matt at the hospital, she also was recovering from post-delivery surgery, which resulted in a roller coaster of hormones and feelings surging through her mind and body. We did not know it at the time, especially since it was so unlike her, but Joyce was experiencing a bout of depression and even terrifying doubts of her ability to be a mother to her newborn twin sons.

It hurts me to think about it, but because of my lack of understanding at the time, Joyce could not share what she was going through with me and was attempting to tough it out until it passed. However, one day Joyce shared what was going through her mind with an older lady at the church whose wisdom and counsel she trusted. This dear lady explained to Joyce that in addition to the physical battle going on in her body, there was also a spiritual battle going on in her mind. Thankfully, this lady knew the Lord and was not constrained by the religious culture of the denominational church we belonged to. Somehow she knew some women who walked in the fullness of the Spirit and persuaded Joyce to go with her so these women could pray for her. Joyce agreed, and when they arrived at the little church where the other ladies were waiting, they ushered her in, sat her in a chair, and then gathered around to pray for her. Joyce was not sure about all that was going on, but she trusted the Lord and afterward knew that the Lord had touched something deep inside her when the other women prayed for her.

The next day, Joyce went to the hospital to hold Matt and Brad for the first time. She was understandably very anxious to finally get to hold her babies. It had been a week since they had been born and she had been allowed to see them through the nursery window but she had not been allowed to touch them. Again, I know this seems strange by today's standards, but it is what they did at the time. They were in incubators and Joyce had been told that even though it was the first time she had been with them, she would only get to hold them when a nurse brought them out of the nursery to a separate room. When Joyce arrived, she spoke to the head pediatric nurse.

"I'm Joyce Graham and I've come to see my twin boys."

"I'm sorry, but this is not a convenient time," the nurse told her curtly. "You will have to come back later."

Joyce was in no mood to put up with that. "Listen to me," she said, her anger about to boil over. "I have not been allowed to touch my babies since they were born, I am their mother, I am also a nurse, I have my doctor's permission, and I am going to see my babies! If you have a problem with that, you can call the doctor."

Of course, the nurse was not going to call the doctor, so she reluctantly arranged for Joyce to put on a cap, a gown, and rubber gloves and go into a room adjacent to the nursery, where someone would bring the babies to her one at a time. While she was waiting in that room and worrying about some of the thoughts that she had experienced, an African-American man came to the door.

"Are you the mother of the twins?" he asked.

"Yes," Joyce answered.

"Well, you are a very special woman," he told her. "God gave you twins because you are special to Him. They will bring the babies to you shortly." Then he left. Joyce was taken aback by what he had said, but she did not have time to think about it because just then a nurse brought Brad to her. Joyce was overcome with love as she inspected every part of his body to make sure that he had all of his parts and that they were all where they should be. Then she went through the same feeling of love and inspection procedure with Matt when they brought him in.

After her time with Matt was over and they returned him to the nursery, Joyce stopped at the head nurse's desk on the way out and said, "I will be back tomorrow. By the way, would you give me the name of the man who is working in the nursery?"

The head nurse looked at Joyce as though she was crazy. "We have no man working in the nursery," she said. "You must be mistaken."

"But I saw him for myself," Joyce insisted. "He was a black man, and he spoke to me."

At this, the head nurse became very incensed and almost shouted at Joyce. "We do not have a man working in the nursery, and especially not a black man!" (Remember, this was 1971 in Fort Worth, Texas.) "If someone was there," she continued, "I will have a talk to the security people about it."

Joyce was puzzled by the nurse's response, but as she left, she felt the Lord say to her, "He was an angel." That was when she knew that the Lord had heard her prayers and those of the ladies who had prayed for her and that He had sent her comfort and peace in her time of need. She was so thankful for His love and mercy and gentle care when she needed it so much and she still has that feeling of peace every time she thinks of it. By the way, the nurse later told Joyce that they never did figure out who it was that Joyce had talked to.

She Felt the Lord Say to Her,
"He Was An Angel."

After several visits to the hospital, and after finally convincing the doctor that she could properly take care of her premature twins, Joyce and I brought Brad and Matt home. Because they were so small they could only hold a small amount of milk, so they had to be fed every two hours, day and night. Whenever they got off their schedule, it meant a feeding every hour as Joyce would feed one, get him to sleep, and then the other one would be ready to eat. Needless to say, Joyce was running on empty most of the time. Thankfully, Cindy was eight when her twin brothers were born and as they grew she became a second mother to them. Like her mother, she loved babies and tended to them with a big sister's loving care. It was also good preparation for her having her own two sons.

These experiences of going to God for direction and comfort and then seeing Him answer our prayers and the prayers of the ladies who prayed for Joyce served to increase our faith and draw us closer to God. Relating those experiences to the church we were in also strengthened our ties to that church and made us feel that this was the place where God wanted us to serve Him for the remainder of our years. After all, we thought, the place where we had received such blessings must be the best place we could possibly be. So we settled back to continue our church activity and my work with the firm. Mike was involved in Scouts; Cindy had school and her music lessons. Matt and Brad were growing and finding new ways every day to bring excitement into our lives. I eventually learned not to laugh when I called Joyce at lunch each day and listened as she described the latest adventure she had had with the twins.

We were in a good place and we could have stayed there for a long time. However, that was not what God had in mind. As I have said before and will say again, to me, our walk with the Lord is a lifetime journey to become more like Christ. We can picture it like a man and a woman who are called by their master to go on a journey to a distant kingdom. They are not told what the journey will hold for them—just that they must travel on the road that is in front of them. As they travel down the road, they encounter many difficulties. Sometimes the road is full of boulders and ditches and even treacherous places that they must pass through. Then they come to a valley where the land is beautiful and full of broad meadows with bountiful grain blowing in the cool breeze that refreshes their bodies. Encouraged by those who live there, they decide to stop, build a home, start a family, and live in this beautiful place. And so they do. They greatly enjoy their life in this place but after a time their master sends a messenger to tell them that they are to leave the place that they are in and continue their journey. Shall they go or shall they stay? Shall they satisfy themselves or shall they obey?

We were in a good place, but God was calling us to a new place in Him. He did this first of all by giving us the experiences that we described earlier and thereby showing us that, even though where we were was a good place, there was more in walking with Him than we had experienced. He then took us into a time of what I call godly dissatisfaction. When I started with the firm, I thought I would stay there for the rest of my career and Joyce and I thought that we would be part of the denominational church we were in for many years to come. But I began to question my commitment to the firm with its great demands upon my time, my energy, and my efforts to the exclusion of other things that I knew the Lord wanted me to do. During this same time I began to compare what we were doing in the denominational church to what I saw in Scripture and I could not reconcile the differences. I felt like a plow horse with blinders just plowing the ground but not seeing the beauty of the whole field. I longed to take off the religious blinders and see the entire field. I realize now that God had put a longing in my heart for more of Him and more expression of Him in our lives.

I Felt Like a Plow Horse with Blinders Just Plowing the Ground But Not Seeing the Beauty of the Whole Field.

I call this time "godly dissatisfaction" to clearly distinguish it from human discontent, for there is a big difference. Many will think that I am just playing with words and that these two phrases are essentially the same thing. Let me explain it like this. By "human discontent" I mean that self-focused emotion in which people are not satisfied with their present condition and they want something to change that will make their life more comfortable. They do not like the way they look so they want to change their looks. They do not like the car they are driving because someone else has a newer car, so they buy a new car that they cannot really afford and then when the newness wears off of it they don't like the fact that they owe so much for it. They do not like the house they live in because someone they know has a bigger house, so they buy a new house that they cannot really afford and a short time later they don't like the fact that they can barely make the payments. Or, worst of all, husbands or wives come to the place where they become discontent with their spouse, they focus on grievances they have with their spouse, and they become restless and eventually find someone else they hope will make them happy. However, shortly thereafter they realize the destruction that their decision brought about in the lives of so many others, including their children, and they are filled with regret and begin again looking for someone else to satisfy their needs. All of these scenarios and many others are centered in trying to temporarily make ourselves look and feel better than we really are. They are centered in having our identity in things that are temporary and will never completely satisfy our desires. In scriptural terms they are all fleshly desires and contrary to God's will. It is our fallen nature working overtime and it is never satisfied.

One day our son Matt was in my office talking to me. During our conversation he asked about a book I had on my desk. The book was The Mortification of Sin by John Owen, a Puritan pastor. In his quick wit and dry sense of humor Matt said, "It sounds like a horror novel." We had a good laugh but then agreed that his assessment was actually accurate when applied to our human nature. It dies hard and fights us as long as we feed it and thus allow it to live. Human discontent is centered in man and is a lack of faith in God and His provision for our lives.

Godly dissatisfaction, on the other hand, is centered in God and His working in our lives. It is a focus on God that says, like Paul, "…I have learned in whatever state I am, to be content: I know how to be abased, and I know how to abound. Everywhere and in all things I have learned both to be full and to be hungry, both to abound and to suffer need. I can do all things through Christ who strengthens me" (Phil. 4:11–13). Paul was focused on Christ. His life was given to be obedient to all that Christ had called him to. It did not matter whether he had a lot or if he had nothing because his circumstances never dictated his life. Pleasing Christ was what mattered to him. He was content no matter what his condition was because he was abiding in Christ and lived his life in accordance with the revelation of Christ that had been given him. Therefore, even when he was "abounding," having no lack and in a good place, when Christ called him to a new place he left everything and followed the Lord's direction. No longer living for himself but living totally for Christ, he had Christ's attitude and spirit of total and complete obedience.

That is the attitude that all of us who belong to Christ should have. Doing all things as unto Christ, we should be content in whatever we encounter while at the same time we desire to know Him more. Content in whatever He has given us to do, but when He calls us to a higher place He prepares us by giving us the desire to change. Joyce and I were content in what we were doing in the church and I was content with my work until the Holy Spirit began to work in us a desire to know Christ more…and thus a desire to leave the past behind as He directed us to a new place.

> *And Jesus, walking by the Sea of Galilee, saw two brothers, Simon called Peter, and Andrew his brother, casting a net into the sea; for they were fishermen. Then He said to them, "Follow Me, and I will make you fishers of men." They immediately left their nets and followed Him. Going on from there, He saw two other brothers, James the son of Zebedee, and John his brother, in the boat with Zebedee their father, mending their nets. He called them, and immediately they left the boat and their father, and followed Him*
>
> MATTHEW 4:18–22

> *As Jesus passed on from there, He saw a man named Matthew sitting at the tax office. And He said to him, "Follow Me." So he arose and followed Him*
>
> MATTHEW 9:9

Chapter Nine

A New Understanding of God

About a year into the transition process of God moving us to new place in Him, Donnie Williamson, my best friend from high school, called to tell me that another high school friend had asked both of us to be pallbearers at his father's funeral. I agreed. On the day of the funeral Donnie picked me up and we made the two-hour trip to our hometown. We attended the funeral, performed our service as pallbearers, and started back to Fort Worth. All the way up and back we talked about the Lord and we were so engrossed in our conversation that we sat in front of my house talking for another two hours. Through it all I witnessed a fire in Donnie's spirit, a spiritual fervor that I had never seen in him before.

When I finally came inside, I kissed Joyce and said, "I don't know what has happened to Donnie, but he has what I am looking for."

As God sometimes does, I did not see Donnie again for another year. By that time I had told the partner in charge of the office that I was leaving the firm and would be looking for a position in industry. He asked me to stay through the busy season and promised that afterward they would help me find a job with one of our clients. Having made the decision to leave the firm, I was looking forward already to moving on and at the same time wondering what lay ahead in our walk with the Lord.

In God's perfect timing, about two or three weeks before the busy season was over, I was at the office late one night when Donnie called and asked if he could come by and talk with me. Of course, I said yes. When he arrived, we immediately began to talk about the Lord and what He was doing in the new church of which Donnie was now a member. As we talked, I asked him questions about this new church. In response to every inquiry, Donnie opened his Bible to a Scripture that specifically answered my question.

Donnie later told me that as he was driving from Dallas to Fort Worth to see me, he pulled off to the side of the road and began to pray about our upcoming conversation. Each time the Holy Spirit reminded him of a specific scripture, Donnie marked its place on the page with a paperclip. As you have probably guessed, these were the very scriptures that Donnie needed to answer my questions. It is amazing what God will do if we just ask for His guidance.

About a week later I got a call from a recruiter about a job that was available at an oil and gas company in Dallas. I went for an interview and the next day accepted the company's very good offer to manage their tax department. This was one of those occasions when in God's time He made things come together quickly (see Isa. 60:22). Within a two-week period, I had a new job that resulted in a period of professional and financial growth and Joyce and I entered a new stage in our church life that resulted in a period of spiritual growth that we did not even know was available to God's children.

Perhaps you can imagine just how difficult a decision it was for us to leave the denomination that we had been a part of for so many years. The change was even more difficult for Joyce because she had not yet heard from the Lord that this was what we should do. To top it off, the first meetings were not in a church building and most of the members were these "strange people from Chicago" praising God in a meeting the likes of which we had never seen before and talking about the Holy Spirit in ways that we had never heard of. It was like another world to us.

At one of those early meetings, the Lord spoke to Joyce from the fourth chapter of John's Gospel: "Woman, believe Me, the hour is coming when you will neither on this mountain, nor in Jerusalem, worship the Father....But the hour is coming, and now is, when the true worshipers will worship the Father in spirit and truth; for the Father is seeking such to worship Him. God is Spirit, and those who worship Him must worship in spirit and truth" (John 4:21, 23–24). Thus, once again, God spoke to Joyce and gave her faith to embrace Him and the place He was leading us to even though she did not understand everything that lay ahead of us.

Shortly after starting this part of the journey, we went with most of the members of the church to a conference of congregations from around the country that were part of this particular segment of the Charismatic movement. Each meeting during the conference was filled with Spirit-led worship and teaching. There was just no comparison of what we were experiencing now to what we previously had believed was all we could expect from church and our Christian life. At every evening service Joyce and I worshiped the Lord as we had never worshiped Him before. Tears of joy streamed from our eyes as the Lord washed us and prepared us for receiving His Word. We did not worry about what other people were doing or what other people might think. We just opened our hearts and spirits to receive every ounce of living water that He was pouring out on us.

At Every Evening Service Joyce and I Worshiped the Lord as We Had Never Worshiped Him Before.

For the next 10 to 12 years we experienced a level of walking with God and with others that we had not even known existed. We came to understand the joy of serving the Lord by serving others out of a heart of thanksgiving and growing in Christ as we worked together to help one another. This included helping friends with needed painting or repairs of their home and then helping them move into the home when it was ready. One time when we were the ones moving into a new house, Joyce woke up very ill on the morning of the scheduled move. We took her to the pastor's house and with the help of 20 or so friends from the church, by 1:00 that afternoon all of the furniture was in place, every box was unpacked, all of the pictures were on the walls, and lunch was on the table. We then brought Joyce home to her new house to rest and get well. And this is just one example of the loving care that was expressed to all of the members of the congregation as we served the Lord by serving the needs of one another.

In the structure of small groups and the atmosphere of "being there" for one another, we developed close friendships that have lasted for over 30 years and have transcended time, distance, and changing circumstances. Among those enduring friendships was our friendship with Leon and Shirley Price. Leon was not my pastor, nor was he part of my particular small group within the church, but Leon became a true friend and an older brother in the Lord. He always gave me wise counsel that was focused on Christ and born out of the wisdom and love that he had gained from his many years of walking with Christ. Our friendship grew even stronger over time as the Lord allowed me to go with Leon as he ministered to churches throughout the country. I watched him minister to people as he spoke into their lives and revealed the love of Christ to them. He was a treasure given by the Lord to so many people for so many years and I am eternally grateful that we were among those who were given the gift of Leon's ministry while he was with us.

The Lord also allowed me to go with Leon on a month-long trip to Kenya. A retired vice president of a major oil company was working with a small group of Kenyan pastors and a local bishop to minister in Kisumu and some surrounding areas. The group included the leader, Leon, a pastor from New Mexico, and me. This was three ministers and a CPA, so I felt very privileged to be there teaching and ministering to people with men who were in full-time ministry.

My first surprise in arriving in Kenya was the national police force and the army-like control they exercised. The second was being assigned to drive one of the cars, which meant driving through Nairobi in a car with the steering wheel on the right side, while operating a standard shift with my left hand. To my utter surprise and relief, I actually made it through the first roundabout that I had ever seen without getting hit or hitting someone else. Surprise number three was driving over the first 25 MPH speed bump on the highway at 40+ MPH. No one had told me about the speed bumps, but I certainly knew to watch for them after that. I had been told about the periodic police roadblocks with the spiked beams across the road, so I was very careful to slowly pull up and do exactly what I was supposed to do until the police motioned us through.

The local pastors we were working with had arranged meetings where two of us would teach and pray for people. On one occasion I was driving with the pastor from New Mexico to a scheduled meeting, when I pulled the car to a stop in front of a road block, obediently waiting for the guards to wave us through. We had been told that we could not take pictures of the national police, but the pastor who was with me forgot and was taking pictures with the expensive new camera that his congregation had given him before he left for Kenya.

Just as I turned toward him, a tall muscular policeman with his rifle on his shoulder walked up to the passenger side of the car, reached in the open window, and grabbed the camera out of the pastor's hands. I immediately got out of the car to try to talk to him, but all he would say in broken English was that we had to see the police chief in the station across the road. As I was driving over to the police station, I thought of the money belt that I was wearing and that, at a minimum, our violation of their rules would cost us some money. As we were standing in front of the station a policeman walked by us and asked, "You got money?" However, when the police chief came out, I explained to him what we were doing, showed him the books and Bibles that we had in the trunk of the car, and earnestly told him how sorry we were. After a few minutes he told the guard to take the film out of the camera and give the camera back to the pastor. With that he turned and walked back into the police station.

While we were waiting for the police chief, I had looked around and had seen some buildings in the back. I thought about the unrest that was going on in Kenya at the time, of the missionaries who had been out at night and had lost their lives trying to help someone, and the missionaries in other countries who faced real danger on a daily basis. I then thought, "We are only here for a month, but we could disappear and no one would ever know what happened to us." But in the end, nothing had happened to us, we were continuing our trip to the meeting, and it had cost us no money. I had been praying continually, but now my prayer turned to one of thankfulness, not only for God's provision in this incident, but also for the many men and women who have been willing to give everything, including their lives, in serving God.

Everywhere I went, I was presented with a stark contrast to the life we live in the United States: seeing a young man who could not walk upright crawl on his hands and knees all the way from his village to a meeting; praying for so many people who had virtually nothing; the joy that I experienced from praying for the child of one of the pastors in their one-room house; driving with Leon to a meeting and having to make sure the car straddled a ditch in the middle of the road leading up to the building; the pastor who lived in a city compound of tin rooms covering a square block; the pastor who rode his bicycle 15 miles one way every day to his job as a schoolmaster, then back home. In all these experiences, I could not help but notice the sharp contrast between what we consider a sacrifice for the Lord and the sacrifices made by those in other countries. By the end of the trip I was thanking God for the privilege of teaching and praying for people in mud and dung buildings. Supporting mission work took on a whole new meaning for me.

Being introduced to the Holy Spirit and then experiencing the release of His working in our lives and seeing His working in the lives of others made Joyce and I realize why the Lord had brought us into this whole new walk with Him. We had known that there was a Holy Spirit because Scripture clearly describes Him and the empowering presence that He should be in our lives. However, belonging to a denomination in which we experienced God's working in our lives but received no teaching concerning the Holy Spirit left us as those who had a form of religion without the Spirit's life-giving power. But now we were seeing and experiencing His physical and spiritual healing and deliverance that brought new life to our walk with God. His enlightenment of Scripture opened our eyes to see the truth of Christ and bring new life to our relationship with Him. Through the enlightenment of the Holy Spirit we began to see that Christ must be the focus of our lives and that Christ must come to have first place in all things. We came to see that our walk with God was not something that we did on Sunday morning, or maybe even a few meetings here and there; rather it must become a lifestyle of living for Him and not for ourselves.

We Began to See that Christ Must Be the Focus of Our Lives and that Christ Must Come to Have First Place in All Things.

You may have noticed that I mentioned some of the manifestations of the Spirit but did not stay there. Receiving the "power" of the Holy Spirit and finding an individual's gifts and calling from the Holy Spirit is the focus of much of the teaching concerning the Holy Spirit's work in the Church. And all sorts of reactions by people to the release of the Holy Spirit's supernatural workings have come to be associated with the parts of the Body of Christ that have embraced the idea of the Spirit's current working in the Church. However, much of such teaching and practice is man-focused rather than Christ-focused with men trying to elevate themselves rather than seeking to serve others and glorify Christ. What we should see is that the Spirit is continuing Christ's work as He seeks not to glorify Himself but to glorify Christ as He takes of what is Christ's and declares it to us (see John 16:13–15). As the Holy Spirit leads us to abide in Christ and as we become more and more like Christ, the manifestations of the Godhead will naturally flow out of our growing relationship with Him. It is not a matter of working up enough faith in our ability or getting to a place of feeling super-spiritual or any other self-focused effort. If we are focused on Christ and abiding in Christ, we will naturally manifest in our thoughts and words and actions His love, His mercy, His grace, and His healing and delivering power. It is not in us; it is in Christ, through the leading of the Holy Spirit.

In reaction to extremes or out of fear or a lack of faith that God can correct human error, many have rejected the present working of Holy Spirit altogether and taken the position that after the apostles, the Holy Spirit was no longer needed and therefore is not currently active. As you can tell, I do not believe that this is what Scripture teaches, nor has it been my experience in my walk with the Lord. I readily admit that there is much in "Spirit-filled" churches that reflects man's reaction to the Holy Spirit rather than the true working of the Holy Spirit, but we should not reject the truth of the Holy Spirit's active working in our lives just because some of that work comes decorated with man-centered ornaments. That is why we must focus on Christ, for it is only in Him that we will find the true truth. He is the way, the truth, and the life (see John 14:6) and it is only by the enlightenment of the Holy Spirit that we will have the ability to see that truth and receive His life.

His life is what we experienced when we came into an understanding of the Holy Spirit as He brought the continuing presence of Christ in us. Instead of feeling that we had to please Him through following rules and regulations, we were set free to walk in relationship with the living God, who gives us His life through the Holy Spirit.

In Him was life, and the life was the light of men

JOHN 1:4

I have come that they may have life...

JOHN 10:10B

"He who believes in Me, as the Scripture has said, out of his heart will flow rivers of living water." But this He spoke concerning the Spirit, whom those believing in Him would receive...

JOHN 7:38–39 (SEE ALSO ISAIAH 12:2–6)

Chapter Ten

The Absolute Necessity of Forgiveness

As God moved us into this new phase of our journey with Him, this new understanding of Him, He began to give us a new understanding of our need to become like Christ. Notice I did not say "complete understanding." As I have said many times, our walk with God is a lifetime process of being transformed by the renewing of our minds so that we may come to know Him more and therefore become more like Him. As a father teaches and trains his sons and daughters through the different stages of their life by giving them understanding of the things they need to know, so our heavenly Father, in Christ, by the Holy Spirit, teaches and trains us as He opens our minds to understand what we need to grow in Him. Thank God that this is a process! Scripture tells us that the old man does not die easily; if we saw in the beginning everything in our lives that needed to change, we would give up in discouragement before proceeding very far or else die in the ensuing battle. But God in

His mercy and love reveals His truth to us at the perfect time and in the perfect way to produce His life in us. He had called us to a new place in Him, but there was a major change that had to take place in me before I could see what He had for us.

Considering how I was raised, I could have blamed my parents, my environment, or a number of other things that I was exposed to for my failures and the issues that I had to deal with. After all, passing the buck is an easy thing to do and it is a convenient cloak that we can use to hide our insecurities and sense of inadequacy.

Outwardly I was an obedient son, but inwardly I was straining to bury my feelings of anger and resentment. However, when my father turned his back on the church and went back to his former way of life, the simmering embers of anger and resentment in me were fanned into a roaring fire that lasted many years. I remember one night when he was out "somewhere," and the thoughts of his way of life and the shame it had brought to our family, caused my anger to boil within me. But still, I did not do anything about it and eventually my feelings receded into a simmering resignation as to who and what he was.

I managed to hide most of my feelings from everyone except Joyce as I tried the best I could to be what I knew I should be. But the effects of my sin of unforgiveness were felt by those I most loved and most wanted to protect. I later came to see that day by day we teach who we really are, rather than who we say we are or pretend to be. The very things we think we have hidden deep inside cry out to those around us in all we do. Our true self, the person we really are internally, is reflected externally even when we try to cover it in religious trappings. Regardless of our efforts otherwise, and except for the grace of God, we eventually will reap what we have sown. Thus it was with me until God was faithful to show me the absolute necessity of forgiveness.

After Joyce and I attended a weekend conference where the speaker spent a significant amount of time talking about forgiveness, the Holy Spirit prompted me to call my mother and father and ask their forgiveness for my attitude concerning my upbringing. Outwardly, I had always been a "loving son," but inside my anger and resentment and unforgiveness burned in my spirit as I held onto the hurts, the disappointments, and the pain of the past. There were those who said that I was justified in my feelings, that God was the only One I needed to deal with, and that I did not need to ask for forgiveness from a father who had done what he did. But I knew that I had to do what the Holy Spirit had told me to do, so I made the call. My parents did not understand what I was doing, but my simple act of obedience to God in letting go of my anger and resentment, my act of repentance in response to the Holy Spirit's prompting, released me to go on with the Lord as He led me to take full responsibility for my sin of unforgiveness and to thereby trust Him to change my heart.

That was the starting point of my coming to understand the absolute necessity of forgiving others no matter how justified I thought I was in not forgiving them. As God began to deal with me more and more on this issue, I learned that unresolved anger will grow into a root of bitterness that will grow into a prison of resentment. Unless the prison door is opened by the key of forgiveness, we will remain there until the dust of our spirit is blown into the pit of despair. That is what would have happened to me if God had not opened the prison door by giving me His grace to forgive. And it is what I have seen happen to so many people who refuse to forgive.

Forgiveness is difficult; our sinful nature fights against it. But we must forgive. Unforgiveness is essentially unrepentant disobedience to God and it will remain an obstacle to our walk with God until we repent, forgive, receive God's forgiveness, and then go on with Him. . We can forgive and go on with God or we can respond to difficult situations by building walls of resentment around ourselves. We think that these walls will protect us from future pain when all they really do is seal us inside while we feed our unforgiveness. Our refusal to forgive keeps us in bondage. Having been blinded by our resentment and unforgiveness, we do not even have the ability to see that we are in bondage, much less have a desire to be released. Our fallen nature blinds us to the truth that the Lord is the only one who can set us free. The longer we stay in bondage, the more our spirit dries up and the more our unforgiveness manifests in spiritual, mental, and physical problems. If we are parents, we pass our unforgiving spirit on to our children.

Unforgiveness is Essentially Unrepentant Disobedience to God.

But glory to God, our Lord Jesus Christ sets us free from our bondage. As Jesus began His public ministry, He defined His purpose this way, quoting from the Book of Isaiah: "The Spirit of the Lord is upon Me, because He has anointed Me to preach the gospel to the poor; He has sent Me to heal the brokenhearted, to proclaim liberty to the captives and recovery of sight to the blind, to set at liberty those who are oppressed; to proclaim the acceptable year of the Lord" (Luke 4:18–19). Initially, Jesus gives us His deliverance, His healing, His sight, and His freedom when He calls us from our spiritual grave into life eternal and opens our eyes to see His Kingdom. It also occurs over the remaining days of our life as we are released from the captivity and oppression and bondage of our fallen nature and are transformed into the nature of Christ.

In Christ, by the Holy Spirit, God in His mercy opens our spiritually blind eyes to see Him. He opens our spiritually deaf ears to hear His loving words of salvation. He reaches down and breaks the chains of our spiritual bondage and delivers us into His marvelous Kingdom of eternal life.

Think about it. Considering my early childhood, is there any natural reason for my being saved from the only life that I knew and brought into a relationship with Christ? Considering that I barely knew there was a God, is there any natural reason why I should be transformed into someone who loves God? Considering that I deserved nothing but eternal damnation, is there any natural reason why God did not exercise righteous judgment but instead pardoned me through the sacrifice of my Lord Jesus Christ, by the power of the Holy Spirit, and granted me eternal life? Not in my mind there isn't. The only explanation is that, as Scripture teaches, we have all been saved by grace through faith and even that faith is not from us, but is the gift of God. Our salvation is not by any works on our part, lest we should boast of anything good coming from us, but it is all from God, through Christ by the Holy Spirit (see Eph. 2:8–9). Having been forgiven so much, how could I do anything but forgive? As Scripture admonishes us to do, I was compelled by the love of Christ, by the understanding of how much I had been forgiven, to forgive even as God in Christ had forgiven me.

As Christ has forgiven us, we must respond to His command for us to truly forgive. Lest we miss the message, He also clearly gave the consequences of not truly forgiving. No one knows how often the model prayer that Christ gave in Matthew 6:5–13 is repeated every day, but Christ also said in verses 14 and 15, "For if you forgive men their trespasses, your heavenly Father will also forgive you. But if you do not forgive men their trespasses, neither will your Father forgive your trespasses." In Matthew 18:21–35, Jesus told the parable of the unforgiving servant who was forgiven a great debt by his master but then would not forgive a small debt that was owed to him by another servant. Jesus concludes the parable by saying that the master called the first servant and said to him, "'You wicked servant! I forgave you all that debt because you begged me. Should you not also have had compassion on your fellow servant, just as I had pity on you?' And his master was angry, and delivered him to the torturers until he should pay all that was due to him. So My heavenly Father also will do to you if each of you, from his heart, does not forgive his brother his trespasses" (Matt. 18:32–35). God has forgiven us much and so we must forgive others.

One last thing I will add: Forgiveness is not a one-time, once-and-for-all activity; we will be presented many, many opportunities to forgive throughout our lifetime. As we grow in Christ, as we mature, we learn to distinguish between those self-focused irritations from which we repent and go on and true offences for which we must extend forgiveness. The former we just do not take personally; and when the latter does occur, we immediately pray for the offender and ask God how we can reflect the heart of forgiveness that He has given us.

It is part of the process of becoming like Christ and so it was with me. In addition to truly forgiving my father, I had to learn to truly forgive friends, family, church leaders, and even myself. I also had to learn the Father's forgiving heart when Mike rebelled under less than ideal circumstances. It was one of the most heart breaking and heart-rending times that we have ever experienced. I agonized through it until I saw the Father's heart to forgive and then saw God restore our relationship with Mike. Each of these times was a new lesson in walking with the Lord and a new lesson in being a conduit for His forgiveness and it will continue throughout the remainder of my life. There is no fixed number of times that we must forgive. Jesus told His disciples: "Take heed to yourselves. If your brother sins against you, rebuke him; and if he repents, forgive him. And if he sins against you seven times in a day, and seven times in a day returns to you, saying, 'I repent,' you shall forgive him" (Luke 17:3–4). Peter apparently thought he had nailed the concept of forgiveness when he asked, "Lord, how often shall my brother sin against me, and I forgive him? Up to seven times?" (Matt. 18:21). He probably was not prepared for Jesus' answer: "I do not say to you, up to seven times, but up to seventy times seven" (Matt. 18:22). Of course, Jesus was not saying that even 490 times was the upper limit of forgiveness, nor was He saying that forgiveness could be reduced to a formula. Forgiveness does not keep track of times. (Aren't you glad that God does not keep track of the number of times we need to be forgiven every day?) As the parable that follows in Matthew 18:23 through 35 tells us, continual true forgiveness from the heart is what matters—and that comes from an understanding that in view of how much we have been forgiven, we must forgive others no matter how many times we have to do so.

In Addition to Truly Forgiving My Father, I Had to Learn to Truly Forgive Friends, Family, Church Leaders, and Even Myself.

It is not about what the other person does; only God can change that person and grant him or her forgiveness. It is about our obedience to God as we respond in love to the love that He had poured out on us. Luke 7:36–50 tells us the story of the sinful woman who washed Jesus' feet with her tears, kissed them, and anointed them with fragrant oil. A Pharisee who was there was, of course, incensed that Jesus would allow this to happen. But Jesus used it to teach that those who are forgiven more will love more. In verse 47 he said, "Therefore I say to you, her sins, which are many, are forgiven, for she loved much. [She understood how much she had been forgiven.] But to whom little is forgiven, the same loves little.[They did not understand.]" As we have been forgiven, so must we forgive.

And do not grieve the Holy Spirit of God, by whom you were sealed for the day of redemption. Let all bitterness, wrath, anger, clamor, and evil speaking be put away from you, with all malice. And be kind to one another, tenderhearted, forgiving one another, even as God in Christ forgave you

EPHESIANS 4:30–32

Chapter Eleven

His Unconditional Love

Our departure from the denominational church that had been our home for years to become part of the church that helped us grow in the knowledge and experience of the Holy Spirit coincided with my departure from the public accounting firm to which I had devoted many years of my life, in order to accept a position at a large oil and gas company in Dallas. This double transition initiated a 12-year period that in many ways was the best of times for us spiritually as well as the best of times for me professionally. After moving to our new church, Joyce and I enjoyed continual growth in the Lord and a new level of prayer, study, teaching, serving, and pure fellowship with others. My new position at the company in Dallas was a time of great professional growth for me. The job was very rewarding both financially and professionally as the company grew in every aspect of its business and generously provided for its employees along the way.

However, from a natural standpoint, the three years that followed were the worst of times for us in both arenas. In our church life, we watched in sorrow and dismay as, after sacrificially giving our time, energy, emotions, and money, including most of our retirement to fulfill a pledge we had made to the Lord (He more than abundantly restored it later), the church began to come apart because of unrighteous leadership. As with many movements throughout the history of the Church, having begun in the Spirit, church leadership changed from focusing on Christ and serving others out of their relationship with Christ, to being focused on themselves and what they could get from the congregation. Many who had started with a vision of building God's Church sold their vision for a position in "their" church. Their focus became one of maintaining the organization and their position rather than one of proclaiming and living Christ. They created an "us against them mentality" in which they were the only ones with the answers. They became like those who ask, "What shall I do with my money? What shall I do with my people? What shall I do with my ministry?" when the questions should have been, "How does God want me to steward His resources? How does God want me to serve His other sons and daughters? How does God want me to exalt Christ in this small part of His work (no matter how large)?" In the end, like so many before them, rather than bringing Christ's life to Christ's people, they surrounded themselves with people who only told them what they wanted to hear and eventually disqualified themselves from being in His service.

This has happened countless times throughout the history of the Church when church leaders do not have the heart and mind of Christ. When they turn from walking in the light of Christ and walk in the light of their own fire, darkness replaces true light and the Spirit is replaced with legalism. However, God saves those who are His and teaches them to look to Him alone rather than looking to men. (See the "I will" statements in Ezekiel chapters 34 through 36.)

At the same time that the church was falling apart, the oil and gas company was acquired by a larger company. Less than six months after the acquisition, the price of natural gas plummeted. The parent company tried to cut its losses, dismantled the company, and I became part of a corporate reorganization that did not include me. Both church and job ended at the same time. Everything that I had given myself to and, in many ways, had drawn my identity from, was coming apart. How could this be happening? The church was the place where we had come to know the presence and power of the Holy Spirit; the place where we had grown so much and had experienced such abundant blessings from God. My job had been good to me and had given me the ability to give above and beyond to the church and to bless other people. How could both the church and my job now be ending?

Everything that I Had Given Myself to and, in Many Ways, Had Drawn My Identity From, Was Coming Apart.

I had, of course, been praying throughout this agonizing process, but I had not heard any response to my cries for help. I felt like my prayers were hitting a stone-cold ceiling and falling back to the ground around my feet. Later on I realized that God had heard and was working on my behalf, but I also realized that I had become so focused on my own circumstances rather than on Christ that I was unable to hear His voice.

With these questions before me and in the midst of both a church demise and the pending change of employment, I came home from work late one night, pulled into my garage, and felt like I could not get out of my car. I sat there for a long time—I don't know how long—just thinking about everything that was going on. Finally, Joyce came out and got me into the house.

At 3:00 the next morning I was in the den crying out to God, "Lord, just say something! I do not care what it is; I just need to hear You." It was then that I heard God say to me in a most fatherly voice, "Steve, My love does not depend on your serving. It does not depend on your giving. It does not depend on your pleasing other people. My love is unconditional." Gracious Lord! I had known about His love intellectually and I knew what Scripture said, but at that moment He wrote His love upon my heart and made the truth of His unconditional love real to me. I had known about His love but now I knew the reality of His love as I had never known it before and it changed my life. Like Job, I proclaimed in my heart, "I have heard of You by the hearing of the ear, but now my eye sees You" (Job 42:5).

God's unconditional love is so fundamental to our understanding of our walk with Him that I cannot tell you why it took so long or such a traumatic experience for the light to finally come on in my heart. I have observed over the years that people only change out of inspiration or desperation but, for me, it was inspiration in the midst of desperation. It was God's perfect timing that I had to come to such a point before the stronghold of conditional love was ready to be broken and the truth of His unconditional love was ready to be planted in my spirit. But thank God it was planted at that moment and it has continued to grow in the ensuing years.

I have also come to see that it was a necessary part of God's working in our lives to bring us to a place where self is broken, where self is emptied, where self is stripped of our narcissistic fig leaves and we acknowledge that only God can provide adequate covering for our spiritual nakedness. We must come to that place before we can understand that there is nothing that we can do to save ourselves; there is nothing that we can do to earn our way to heaven; there is nothing that we can do to earn His love; it is freely given, unconditional love. Do we enjoy what we have to go through in that place? No, we don't. But when He shows us His love as He takes us through that place, we come to see that it is in the darkest times of our lives that we can see His most brilliant light. It is in the times when we are carrying our greatest burdens that we can see His great strength lifting those burdens from our shoulders. It is in the times when we are at our lowest that we can experience His love raising us up to sit with Him in heavenly places. It is in the times when we are empty that we turn to God and are filled with the fullness of His love.

It is in the Times When We are Empty that We Turn to God and Are Filled with the Fullness of His Love.

Paul's dramatic conversion from a "Pharisee of Pharisees" who persecuted the Church to the apostle to the Gentiles led him to know the love of Christ as few others have before or since. In his letter to the Ephesians, he prayed for all of us that "He would grant you, according to the riches of His glory, to be strengthened with might through His Spirit in the inner man, that Christ may dwell in your hearts through faith; that you, being rooted and grounded in love, may be able to comprehend with all the saints what is the width and length and depth and height—to know the love of Christ which passes knowledge; that you may be filled with all the fullness of God" (Eph. 3:16–19).

Can you imagine how overcome Paul must have been as he realized that when he was at war with Christ, when he was totally contrary to Christ, when he was putting Christ's followers to death, Christ extended His love to Paul and made him an apostle? As he realized that such love was totally undeserved and totally unconditional and totally beyond his natural ability to understand, he could not help but pray that all of the saints would come to know such love.

Paul's upbringing, religious culture, and training as a "Pharisee of Pharisees," combined with his dramatic conversion to Christ on the road to Damascus, provided the background for the focus of his preaching, his teaching, and his prayers. Having once followed every jot and tittle of the law, he now urges us to live in Christ's love, not legalism; having once followed God by adhering to rules and regulations, he now urges us to abide in Christ and live in total submission to Him. As a former persecutor of the Church who had agreed to the deaths of Christians, Paul understood that it was Christ's love that chose him and forgave him. As a result, he understood the importance of all the saints understanding how much Christ loves us so that we might thereby love Him in return. As John wrote, "We love Him because He first loved us" (1 John 4:19). Because of his dramatic conversion and the changes in his life brought about by the Holy Spirit, Paul understood the changes of heart, mind, and spirit needed by all Christians, and he prayed without ceasing for the spiritual growth of all the saints, that they might understand the love of Christ as a key to their growth in Christ.

Paul prays that Christ's love would be so completely fixed in our spirits that it would become like a well-founded building or a deeply planted tree. By these two metaphors of Christ's indwelling in us through His love, he tells us that the roots of Christ's love must be so deeply planted in our hearts and our foundation in Christ's love so firm that nothing will shake us. If His love is so established in our spirits as to be like a solid foundation or a deeply rooted tree, we will be able to withstand the storms of life and walk in Christ's victory. Then we will sing with the saints of old, "On Christ the solid Rock I stand, all other ground is sinking sand." (See Matthew 7:24–27.)

Paul knows that the love of Christ cannot be measured by any known earthly measurements and that Christ's love is inexpressible. Nevertheless, he prays that we will understand with all the saints that Christ's love is wide enough to reach the whole world and long enough to encompass all of time from beginning to end. He prays that we understand that the love of Christ is high enough to seat us together with Him in heavenly places and deep enough to reach to the depths of sin's hold on us and require that we be released from Satan's grasp.

Oh, to come to that place where we understand that Christ's love is wide enough to reach even someone who was raised in or is living in the worst of conditions; that it is long enough to save us no matter at what point in life we may be; that it is high enough to raise us from the darkest place to the heights of seeing from His eternal perspective; that it is deep enough to reach us no matter how far we have fallen and no matter how much we are resisting Him! His love is unconditional, everlasting, and able to go beyond our understanding in order to make us His.

For God so loved the world that He gave His only begotten Son, that whoever believes in Him should not perish but have everlasting life

JOHN 3:16

As the Father loved Me, I also have loved you; abide in My love

JOHN 15:9

But God demonstrates His own love toward us, in that while we were still sinners, Christ died for us

ROMANS 5:8

Chapter Twelve

Transformed Marriage

You can probably imagine that the turmoil of the church demise, the job change, and all the other things that happened at the same time put more than just a little stress on our marriage. To see 15 years of giving and serving come to nothing, feeling deeply betrayed by those whom we had trusted to be "men of God," and at the same time to have a very good job of 15 years come to an end, not only tore at our hearts but also at our relationship with each other.

Joyce and I were at a crisis point in our marriage. Both of us were trying to deal with everything in our own way rather than facing it together, each licking our own wounds instead of turning to God together. At one point we were not communicating at all as a married couple. Each of us was reacting to the pressure in accordance with our own personality and nature, expressing our frustration in ways that hit directly on the other's "hot buttons," which only served to compound the conflict. My response was to retreat into my man cave; Joyce's was to attack as she cried out to communicate. We had reached a critical crossroads in our marriage that, except for the Lord's direct intervention, would have led us to divorce.

When the emotional conflict had grown almost to the point of no return, I asked Joyce if she would agree to go to an Arkansas lake cabin that was owned by our dear friends, Leon and Shirley Price. For several years they had graciously allowed us to go to the cabin when we needed to get away from things, and it had become a place where we could rest, relax, and recoup when we really needed it. When people ask me what I did at a lake cabin without TV and a telephone, I would tell them that I would get up early in the morning, eat breakfast, get a cup of coffee, go out on the deck, put my feet up on the rail, and watch the sun come up. Then, a while later, I would watch the sun go back down again. This time, however, I honestly did not know what the trip would lead to; I just knew that we had to get away from the intensity of the situation and see if we could find God in a quieter place.

Joyce did not want to go anywhere with me, especially to a place where it would be just the two of us. Nevertheless, she agreed to give it a try and wait to see if God would say anything while we were there. So we left Fort Worth and started on the eight-hour trip to the cabin. It did not take long for things to start going wrong. We were a couple of hours into Arkansas when our car's transmission suddenly went out while we were driving down the highway. Neither of us was feeling all that great about the trip to begin with; now we had car trouble. Even worse, it was 104 degrees that day. This was before the days of cell phones, so we couldn't just call for help.

Neither of Us was Feeling All that Great About the Trip to Begin With; Now We Had Car Trouble.

Fortunately, the breakdown occurred right at an exit, so I decided to let the car roll to a stop at the entrance to the exit ramp. A short time later, a man stopped and agreed to push the car up the exit ramp and up to the road crossing the highway. I do not know why I did not just ask for a ride to the next town; I guess I thought that someone would come by on the crossroad and give us a hand. We had not been there very long when an old green car, rust spots showing, and obviously not a "top of the line" vehicle, came down the road, pulled over, and stopped. The driver was a woman.

"Can I help you?" she asked.

"Our car broke down," I replied. "I think it's the transmission."

"My cousin runs the local wrecker service. If you'd like, I'll take you to his grandmother's house. She will arrange for him to pick up your car and take you to the next town."

We agreed. As Joyce and I sat down in the backseat, we noticed that the inside of the car was much worse than the outside. That did not matter to us, however; we were just thankful for her help. She took us to "Grandma's" house to arrange for the wrecker service. We met "Grandma," then sat down to wait for the young man who operated the wrecker service. I had noticed the very nice, brand-new wrecker parked in the front yard, and thought, "This won't be too bad after all."

Joyce and I sat down on the couch ready to settle into a pleasant conversation. However, just then, and much to our surprise, Grandma's pet fox darted behind our backs, nipping me as he went by. Joyce immediately got up and went to sit in a chair next to Grandma. Being a man, I of course continued to sit on the couch, determined to act as though nothing was wrong, even though the fox continued to run behind my back and nip at me. Needless to say, I was much relieved when the young man arrived!

When we explained our situation, he said he would be glad to drive us to Arkadelphia, drop our car off at a repair shop, and take us to a motel. As he went outside to start up his big new wrecker, Joyce and I got ready to say our good-byes to Grandma. However, a few minutes later, the young man came back into the house looking embarrassed and rather frustrated. "I don't know what's wrong," he said," but that truck won't start. I'll have to go to my shop to get my old one."

Once again we went back inside to enjoy some more conversation with Grandma and to tolerate her pet fox. When the young man returned, Joyce and I quickly thanked Grandma for her hospitality and climbed into the wrecker. Now, instead of riding in the bright new wrecker, as I had anticipated, we found ourselves in a very old, somewhat dirty truck that had seen its better days, but, thankfully, still worked quite well. Joyce had to sit on my lap as the truck only had one bench seat and the gear shift coming up from the floor prevented anyone from sitting in the middle. We stopped long enough to pick up the car and then headed to Arkadelphia, trying not to look at the hula dancer doll stuck on the dashboard, as she shook from side to side.

During our conversation with the young man, we found out that he and his wife had been married several years and, although they wanted children, had not had any. He said that they were now thinking of starting the in-vitro process. When we got to the motel, and before we got out of the truck, I decided to take a chance.

"Joyce and I have prayed for childless couples several times, and each time God has blessed them with the child they desired. Could we pray for you and your wife and ask the Lord to let her become pregnant?"

"Yes," the young man replied. "I'd be grateful."

We offered up a brief prayer to the Lord, blessed the young man, and then got out of the truck and checked into the motel. He went on his way.

Since the car dealer was closed when we got there, we did not have transportation, so we walked to the closest café (a catfish place) and had dinner. As we waited on our food to arrive, we looked at each other and began to laugh at how ridiculous our situation was. Our mood began to change and we began to think that this might be a good trip after all. The "old fox" had been nipping at us, and had even taken a big bite in a couple of places, but we had been given the opportunity to pray for a stranger and know that God was going to suddenly make Himself real to a young man and his wife.

The next day we walked to the car dealer, arranged for the repairs, and rented the only available car they had. We then packed our suitcases, put them in the car, and drove to the cabin where, we hoped, God would meet us and give us hope for the future.

After arriving at the cabin, we talked about everything we were dealing with and then had a husband/wife prayer meeting. God met us in a supernatural way as the Holy Spirit gave us words to hold onto. As Joyce was praying, the Lord told her that it was not our differences that were causing our conflict, but our similarities; specifically, our strong personalities. He then gave her a vision of a ribbon, gently but purposefully floating in the air. As the ribbon moved through the air, it formed a perfect bow with perfect loops, a perfect knot with both ends of the ribbon extending perfectly from the knot. The Lord then told her that it was at the knot where the ribbon was brought together, where the ribbon was at its closest, and it was what provided the bow's strength. He told her that He was forming us into the bow that He wanted to adorn the life He had for us. It was the knot of this bow where we would be the closest, where both our strong personalities would come together, and where we would find the strength of our marriage.

It was Not Our Differences that Were Causing Our Conflict, But Our Similarities.

In the past, we had thought that it was a place that was confining and unbearable to us as individuals, but it was a place that was absolutely necessary to the beautiful marriage bow that He was forming. If we would yield ourselves to Him, if we would see it as a place of yielded communication between us, if we would see it as a place of unity, it would become the point of strength that formed the bow that He was making.

As Joyce shared this vision that the Lord had given her, the Holy Spirit began to work in both of us, instructing us and giving us wisdom and insight into what He was doing and where He was leading us. Praise and thankfulness filled the rest of the evening as it overflowed from what He had shown us. Did it change what we were going through? No, but it changed us and gave us the faith to work through what was ahead of us. As we reflect on this experience today we are thankful that the Lord does whatever it takes to prepare us to hear from Him. We are also thankful for His showing us that in a crisis situation, a lasting solution will come only when we focus on Him rather than on ourselves and yield ourselves to Him rather than insisting on our own way.

Returning home after God had gotten our attention, we began the healing process of continually reminding ourselves to focus on Jesus, asking for faith to forgive and look forward to what He had for us, and actually thanking Him for the crisis that had been the catalyst for this healing process. We had already realized that we had some obstacles to overcome and some excess baggage to get rid of, but having had no real pattern to follow and being married so young, we had to start with basics rather than build on a proper foundation, which neither of us had received while growing up. We had learned a lot through our years of going to church and hearing numerous teachings on marriage and family, but there still remained root issues that needed to be removed from our thinking. I do not have the space in this book to discuss everything in detail, and since all the marriage guides and books that have been written would cover a small country (or maybe a large one), it is not necessary to do so. Therefore, I will just share the foundational issue that God led us to focus on.

When we consider God as Father, Son, and Holy Spirit, it is good to study and understand the distinctive attributes of each. However, this distinctiveness must be viewed in the context of God's oneness, of His unity. Deuteronomy 6:4 tells us, "Hear, O Israel: The Lord our God, the Lord is one!" He is the only true God and oneness or unity is God's nature; it is part of who He is and it must be reflected in all that He does. In John 10:30, Jesus declared, "I and My Father are one." And in John 17 He prays that those who are His shall be one just as He and the Father are one. It is Jesus' oneness with the Father that provided the basis for His saying or doing only that which He saw or heard or received from His Father. It is the oneness of the Holy Spirit with the Father and the Son that provided the basis for Him to speak not on His own authority, but to speak only what He hears and thereby glorify Christ and not Himself. It is the oneness of the Godhead that is expressed by Paul in calling the Church to unity in Ephesians 4:1–6: "I, therefore, the prisoner of the Lord, beseech you to walk worthy of the calling with which you were called, with all lowliness and gentleness, with longsuffering, bearing with one another in love, endeavoring to keep the unity of the Spirit in the bond of peace. There is one body and one Spirit, just as you were called in one hope of your calling; one Lord; one faith, one baptism; one God and Father of all, who is above all, and through all, and in you all."

Because oneness is God's nature, it is therefore also His design and command for our relationship with Christ, for our relationship with God's other sons and daughters, and in our marriage relationship with our spouse. It is God's design that a man and a woman shall be one in marriage. However, since it is our nature to be independent, to rebel against authority, and to be contrary to God, oneness is not a concept that we readily embrace, much less practice. And because of the closeness of a husband and wife relationship, oneness is even more difficult in marriage.

We must work at it continually. We must study continually and apply what we learn continually if we are to achieve God's oneness in our marriage.

In doing so, it is good to understand the differences between the way men and women think and respond to different situations and to understand the differences in the fundamental needs of a man in contrast to the fundamental needs of a woman. However, the distinctiveness of a man and the distinctiveness of a woman must be viewed in the context of God's nature of oneness and, therefore, of His design for our oneness in marriage. When God instituted marriage, He said that a man and a woman should no longer be separate, but in marriage should be one.

I know that the concept of oneness in marriage sounds strange in a culture where men and women generally seek only what they think is best for themselves as separate individuals. In doing this we are only following our basic nature, which is to be self-focused in everything we do. Add to this the man's nature to abdicate his responsibility to be the spiritual head of his family and the woman's nature to want her husband's place of leadership, and the difficulty of following God's design for oneness in marriage becomes apparent.

Impossible to achieve by our own efforts, the unity that God designed for marriage as signified by oneness must begin with and be born out of each partner's oneness with Christ. Romans 8:29 tells us that we who are children of God are predestined to be conformed to the image of Christ. As we give ourselves to being conformed to Christ's nature by the Holy Spirit's transforming power, we become more like Christ and reflect His love and mercy and grace and faithfulness to each other. As each spouse abides more and more in Christ, His nature of oneness becomes our nature and we thus desire oneness with each other. Out of a husband's and wife's oneness with Christ comes their oneness with each other.

Out of a Husband's and Wife's Oneness with Christ Comes Their Oneness with Each Other.

This takes a lifetime of growth in our relationship with Christ and a resultant lifetime of growth in our relationship with each other. It is not what we would do naturally, but it is the only way that we will experience the true love, the true peace, the true joy, and the true blessing that God intended for marriage. It is the only way a man can be the husband and the father that he should be and the only way that a woman can be the wife and mother that she should be. It is the only way that the oneness, the unity, that is the nature of God can be expressed in marriage, in family, and then in the Body of Christ.

This is not a process of "losing our identity," which is so fearful to many people, but it is a process of finding our true identity in Christ as our will is conformed to the will of Christ. God created each of us to be a distinct individual and we uniquely reflect His nature in the way that He created us. But God designed the uniqueness of a woman and the uniqueness of a man to be brought together in marriage so that each one shall be made complete as one in Christ, to bring glory to Him. It is when our separateness is brought to that place of being joined together as one in Christ that the full strength of two made one is revealed. As long as a husband and wife remain separate, they are like the two ends of the ribbon being pulled in different directions. But when they come together as God designed, as they recognize and honor each other as "heirs together of the grace of life" (1 Pet. 3:7), they then reflect the beauty of God's creation and thereby bring glory to Him.

> ... "Have you not read that He who made them at the beginning 'made them male and female,' and said, 'For this reason a man shall leave his father and mother and be joined to his wife, and the two shall become one flesh'? So then, they are no longer two but one flesh. Therefore what God has joined together, let not man separate"
>
> MATTHEW 19:4–6

Chapter Thirteen

Not My Will, But Yours Be Done

Not long into the process of working through the aftermath of the church demise and job change and focusing on the Lord rather than ourselves, Joyce and I were confronted with another life-changing experience. One day while I was at work and Joyce was at home, Brad came by the house to get a few things and then head back to college on Matt's motorcycle. (They roomed together at school.) Just as he was leaving, Joyce was prompted by the Holy Spirit to pray for his safety. Only a few blocks from the house, a young man with drugs and alcohol in his system, and more in his car, turned left in front of Brad. In Brad's words, "I hit the right rear passenger's door head-on. I was launched over the car. I could see the luggage rack on top. The rack was chrome against a green car top." Brad flipped over the car and, again, in his words:

My left heel hit the ground, then my chest and head. Then I noticed my left foot awkwardly pressed against the facemask of my helmet. I then rolled several times in many configurations until I landed face up, on my back, with my left leg tucked unnaturally back and under my right leg. I could feel nothing. When the paramedics got there and started working on me, I could feel them moving my legs, but there was no pain. As they cut my pants free, I began to have sensations starting from the top of my head as if my entire body had fallen asleep. As the sensation returned slowly from head to toe, I braced for it as I anticipated it reaching my left leg, which I could tell took the brunt of the impact. As my brain and knee connected, it felt as though a railroad nail was driven through my knee joint. This was when I realized the extent of my injury.

When Joyce arrived, the paramedics told her that Brad was probably not hurt very badly as there was no blood or any other outward appearance of damage. But she knew differently when Brad, who was a "pain passes" guy, looked up at her and said, "Mom, my knee is messed up *bad!*"

I normally would have worked late that day, but when Joyce called and told me that Brad had been injured, I got in the car and started to the hospital where Brad had been taken. It was late afternoon rush hour, however, and the freeway was full of cars moving at about five miles an hour with stop-and-start traffic most of the way. After putting up with this for a little while and thinking constantly of my son being in the hospital, I did something that was totally out of character for me. I pulled over to the left between the inside lane and the road divider, put on my blinkers, and proceeded to drive as fast as I dared to pass the other cars. When I got close to the hospital exit, I put on my right turn signal and prayed that someone in each of the three lanes that I had to cross would let me over to the exit. Maybe they saw the look on my face or realized that I was in a hurry to get to the hospital, but cars in each lane stopped and let me through.

When I got to the emergency room, I learned that X-rays revealed just how right Brad had been about his injury. One of the doctors explained it to us. "Brad's left tibia is broken in 32 pieces, crushed by the internal impact of his femur. The largest broken piece has a jagged edge, which, had it cut the main artery in his leg, he probably would've have bled out before we could have gotten to it. Frankly, his leg is in a mess, and we are not sure we can put it back together. Even if we can, we probably will have to fuse Brad's knee or, failing that, amputate his leg above the knee."

Upon hearing this news, Brad told us that if fusing his knee was the medical conclusion, he wanted his leg to be amputated. Although we were never totally comfortable with the doctors and with what they had told us, we agreed to the operation that they recommended. Thankfully, God had something else in mind.

Twice the scheduled surgery had to be postponed because a nurse had given him something to eat or drink the night before or there was a conflict with scheduling. After the second postponement, and having doubts about the surgeons' ability to address Brad's specific injury, we knew that we needed to ask God for clear direction as we reassessed everything. Within a few hours of making that decision, we received a call from a friend at church who reminded us that another member of the church managed a hospital in Dallas that he jointly owned with a group of doctors. She suggested that we call him to see if he might be able to help Brad. I called him immediately.

After I explained the situation, he said, "The doctors who practice at my hospital do not service Brad's kind of injury, but I know doctors who do. As soon as we hang up I will call some Dallas bone and joint doctors I know and see if they will agree to take a look at Brad's injury."

Not long after, I got word that the doctors he called agreed to change their schedule, so we took Brad to Dallas to see them. One of the doctors was a former surgeon for the U.S. Olympic ski team and the other was a top joint surgeon in Dallas. They gave us essentially the same prognosis as we had been given before, but it was obvious that they knew exactly what they were doing and they gave us some hope for the best outcome under the circumstances.

The surgery was scheduled and the night before it was to be performed, we checked Brad into the hospital in Dallas. I will let Brad describe what happened in his own words:

> As I lay in the hospital bed, I prayed and asked God to be free from the process that I knew was ahead of me. I had been through knee surgery before on my right knee, but I knew that this would be much worse. I prayed, stepped out of bed, and stood on both legs with no pain. However, before I took a step, I know that I heard God tell me that instant healing was not my path and I was required to take the harder road, that He was more interested in what needed to be done in me rather than for me. God is more interested in the individual than He is in the desires of the family or the faith of the masses—and that may not mean immediate physical healing.

"He was More Interested in What Needed to Be Done in Me Rather than For Me."

We, of course, had been praying from the start, but there was still a hint of helplessness as we arrived early that morning for the surgery. Time crawled until the joint surgeon came out of the operating room to talk to us. We could tell by the very concerned look on his face that all was not well.

"I'm sorry, but Brad's bones are just not coming together. It looks as though we will have to fuse his knee."

Upon hearing what the doctor said, we did not think about preferences or alternatives; we just knew that we had to pray. Joyce sat down in a chair and began to pray, but the Holy Spirit led me to fall on the floor of the surgery waiting room and cry out to Him in prayer. I do not remember, and did not care at the time, but Joyce said that the two people who were in the waiting room with us got up and left. To me it seemed like only 30 minutes or so, but Joyce said that it was an hour and a half later when the joint surgeon came out again.

"I don't understand it," he said, "but the bones just suddenly came together like a puzzle. After rehab, Brad should be able to walk again."

You can imagine how overwhelmed with joy and relief we were by this news!

Brad's operation was followed by excruciatingly painful rehab (a whole story in itself) and then a full recovery. In fact, when the doctors went back in to remove the metal and screws that had been used to hold the bones together, they were amazed to see that even the torn cartilage had grown back. The knee surgeon told us that he rarely stitched cartilage together because, due to a lack of blood supply, it normally does not regenerate, but in Brad's case, for some reason, he did sew the cartilage back together and it had regenerated.

Brad later got the metal pieces and screws from the doctor and had them framed with a plaque at the bottom that reads, "I walk not by the power which is made by man but by the healing power of God." It now hangs in his office at work. We are so thankful that the Lord gave us the faith to pray, that He led us to pray during the operation, and that He showed us what to pray for. We are, of course, thankful for Brad's healing, and as the words on the plaque indicate, we give God the glory for the outcome. However, when we go through something as traumatic as this was, we must step back and ask ourselves what we learned from it rather than just taking what might have touched us emotionally.

As we did that after this experience, we concluded that the most significant thing was Brad's perspective of his encounter with God. When Brad heard God say that he would not be healed immediately but instead would have to take "the harder road" and go through the operation, Brad could have been overwhelmed with disappointment and filled with discouragement. Instead, he accepted God's word as not only "the harder road" but also "the higher road" that led him to a new understanding of God. I will let Brad give you his perspective:

God's plan was not to heal me instantaneously but for the surgery to be successful. I knew this the night before as I stood beside my hospital bed. My answer had already been provided and the outcome had already been determined. The prayers that were offered to God on my behalf may have been in accordance with God's will, but His will had already been determined. To me, the answer could just as easily have been amputation. If it had been amputation, I do not think the rehab would have been any harder. I know that I would not have had a second surgery, nor would I have had the potential for a knee replacement as a real possibility sometime in the next 20 years. Looking back, I am really indifferent to the outcome. The significance to me is that for the first time in my life, I was at peace with whatever was required of me.

The significance was that Brad was at peace regardless of the outcome. For the first time he was at peace in saying, "Not my will, but Yours be done." Regardless of the outcome, God is still God.

Regardless of the Outcome, God is Still God.

As with all things, our Lord Jesus Christ is the perfect example as He fell on His face and prayed, "O My Father, if it is possible, let this cup pass from Me; nevertheless, not as I will, but as You will" (Matt.

26:39). Knowing what was ahead of Him, knowing what He must suffer, knowing that those who had been closest to Him would be scattered and leave Him alone (see Matt. 26:31; John 16:32), in His humanity Jesus was "exceedingly sorrowful" and "deeply distressed." (Matt. 26:37–38). As He fell on His face to pray, He knew that His Father would be with Him, He knew that He would never be separated from His Father's love, He knew that His Father could make the cup pass from Him, but desiring only to be obedient to the Father's will He submitted to that will and rested in the knowledge that His Father was sufficient for anything that was ahead of Him. But He was one with His Father and, in my view, the foreshadow of even a moment's separation from His Father in the midst of the spiritual darkness that fell upon the cross as He took on the sins of the world brought agony to His spirit. As He prayed more earnestly, His sweat became like great drops of blood falling to the ground. He had come in obedience to the Father, everything He did was in obedience to the Father, and in His great time of anguish He prayed in obedience to the Father, saying, "…nevertheless, not as I will, but as You will."

We do not understand how, but Jesus was at peace as He went forward with the outcome in His Father's hands (see Matt. 26:36–46; Mark 14:32–42; Luke 22:39–46; John 16:32).

Having the Spirit of Christ, Paul tells us in 2 Corinthians 12:7–10, "And lest I should be exalted above measure by the abundance of the revelations, a thorn in the flesh was given to me, a messenger of Satan to buffet me, lest I be exalted above measure. Concerning this thing I pleaded with the Lord three times [like his Lord Jesus in the garden] that it might depart from me. And He said to me, 'My grace is sufficient for you, for My strength is made perfect in weakness.' Therefore most gladly I will rather boast in my infirmities, that the power of Christ may rest upon me. Therefore I take pleasure in infirmities, in reproaches, in needs, in persecutions, in distresses, for Christ's sake. For when I am weak, then

I am strong." And then in Philippians 4:6–7 he tells us, "Be anxious for nothing, but in everything by prayer and supplication, with thanksgiving, let your requests be made known to God; and the peace of God, which surpasses all understanding, will guard your hearts and minds through Christ Jesus." Be anxious for nothing; not for anything, regardless of the circumstances. Pray with thanksgiving in everything; in everything, regardless of the circumstances.

How could Paul say these things that seem so strange and foreign to most who hear them? How could a man who experienced beatings, prison, shipwrecks, danger, weariness, sleeplessness, hunger and thirst, cold and heat without adequate clothing, and at times homelessness (see 2 Cor. 11:22–33) say all these things? He labored with his own hands, he was spoken of with contempt, but he blessed in return. He was persecuted, but he endured; he was slandered, but he exhorted all to believe in Christ. He said that he was "made as the filth of the world, the offscouring of all things" (1 Cor. 4:13), yet he said, "be anxious for nothing" and "in everything" pray "with thanksgiving" and "the peace of God, which surpasses all understanding, will guard your hearts and minds through Christ Jesus." Our human nature cannot understand this insight. Our natural minds fight against it and only seek what is best from our standpoint. But Paul knew the peace of God that passes our natural understanding because he was focused on Christ and not himself and therefore he faced all things in God's grace, giving thanks for all things that he encountered in his service to Christ.

Jesus came in total obedience to the Father. He was totally focused on pleasing His Father. Therefore He looked solely to His Father for direction and then acted in accordance with His Father's will. Paul said that he had been crucified with Christ and therefore no longer lived, but Christ lived in him. By faith he desired to say and do only that which was in obedience to Christ. By the love of the Father, by the sacrifice of

Christ, through the power of the Holy Spirit, Paul had been transformed from one who was at war with God to one who gave his all for God. His faith was in Christ alone; he looked to Christ alone, who was the source of his faith; and everything he did was focused on pleasing Christ alone. Out of his abiding in Christ, like Christ, Paul looked upward for direction and then outward for application of God's will as he laid down his life for the Church.

It did not matter what Paul endured. Neither the circumstances that Paul faced nor what would happen to him in those circumstances dictated his perspective, for he had the mind of Christ. He knew God, he walked in obedience to the Lord, and therefore he could walk in the peace of Christ that passes all natural understanding. In turn, Paul could call all of us to walk in the peace that he knew was available to all of us in Christ. All of us are called to the place where we are to die to our own desires, our concerns for our own comfort, and our own pride and to live for Christ in obedience to His will. Then we will walk in the peace of Christ and be able to say, "No matter the circumstances, no matter the outcome, God is still God and I will trust in Him and Him alone and I will lift my prayers of thankfulness to the Sovereign God of all. No matter what the circumstances, not as I will, but as You will."

> Yet in all these things we are more than conquerors through Him who loved us. For I am persuaded that neither death nor life, nor angels nor principalities nor powers, nor things present nor things to come, nor height nor depth, nor any other created thing, shall be able to separate us from the love of God which is in Christ Jesus our Lord
>
> ROMANS 8:37–39

Part Three

Extraordinary Calling

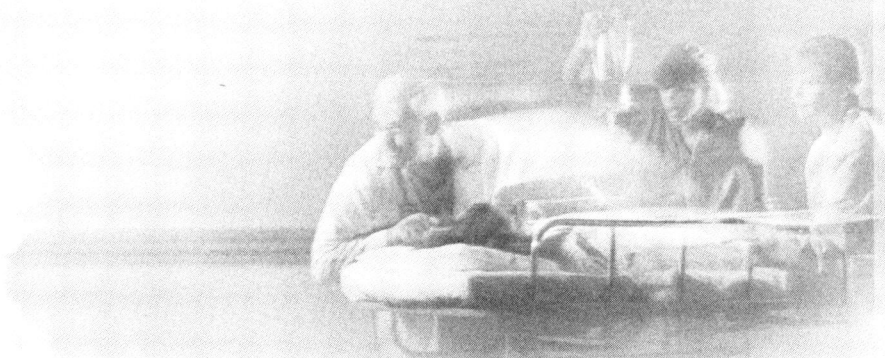

Chapter Fourteen

Pressing On to Know Christ

After the Lord had taken me through a review of His faithfulness to us in the past, He then said, "Steve, as you remembered My faithfulness, what was the primary truth that I called you to?" That was a difficult question. Joyce and I have experienced so many examples of God's faithfulness as we have walked together with Him over mountaintops and through valleys. What was the overriding thought that He has spoken into our lives? What has He taught us through our experiences as He revealed more of Himself to us? As we considered these questions, Joyce and I both agreed that in all things that we encounter in this lifetime journey of becoming like Christ, whether facing a crisis or enjoying a victory that He gave us or doing ordinary things in ordinary ways, we must focus on Christ. And as we walk with Him through all of these things, as we keep our eyes on Christ, we must overcome the challenge of stopping before we complete the journey and press on to know Him more.

This is not a new challenge; Christians of every generation have struggled with the temptation of quitting before the end of their journey, of stopping short of God's perfect will and desire for them. The Book of Hebrews was written to challenge and encourage believers who were considering giving up and ceasing to follow Christ. Setting forth the supremacy of Christ above all that they might otherwise turn to, the writer likens the Christian life to a race that we all must run, encouraged by those who've gone before us, and with our eyes fixed on Jesus: "Therefore we also, since we are surrounded by so great a cloud of witnesses, let us lay aside every weight, and the sin which so easily ensnares us, and let us run with endurance the race that is set before us, looking unto Jesus, the author and finisher of our faith, who for the joy that was set before Him endured the cross, despising the shame, and has sat down at the right hand of the throne of God" (Heb. 12:1–2). In His life of complete obedience to the Father, Jesus was ever tempted to accept a lesser course, but as our supreme example in all things He completed all that the Father had given Him to do exactly as the Father had given Him to do it. The apostles, chosen and trained by Christ, deserted Christ and "went back to fishing." But when they saw the risen and ascended Christ and had been filled with the Holy Spirit, they overcame all obstacles and obediently completed all that He had called them to do. They were followed by the multitude of God's sons and daughters who have overcome the temptation to stop and have instead obediently completed their journey.

There were also many times when Joyce and I could have stopped and not continued on. There were so many times when we could have said, "It is just not worth it." But God called us forward and we continued our journey. When we married so young and faced so many difficulties in working to finish school, it would have been easier from a natural perspective for us simply to stop and not pay the cost of going on. But we would not have learned to persevere in the natural and then understand that in doing so the Holy Spirit was preparing us to persevere spiritually. And we would not have realized that not paying the cost then would have cost us so much more in the long run. From a natural perspective it would have been easier to remain in the denominational church that we had been part of for so long and not step out into unknown territory. But if we had not gone forward, we would never have experienced the joy of knowing the Holy Spirit; the joy of serving Christ through serving others; the release that came through seeing His forgiveness, His righteousness, and His holiness; and the joy of dying to self and living for Christ as the Holy Spirit illuminated Christ to us. We would not have come to see that our walk with Him is not following rules and regulations but is a relationship with Christ; it is not following man's laws but is living in the love of Christ; it is not following a man-centered philosophy but is being guided by Christ-centered truth. And certainly after experiencing within such a short period of time the devastation of unrighteous leadership that led to the demise of the church to which we had given so much, the change of employment, the crisis of Brad's accident and knee surgery, and pressure that threatened to destroy our marriage, we could have turned our back on God and given up. But, had we done so, we would never have understood His unconditional love for us, His faithful provision for us in all things, the oneness and unity of God, the opportunity for systematic study of His Word that came out of that traumatic time, or the revelation of God and His Church that could only come to us from going through such an experience.

And, after having a sudden cardiac arrest at my age, even with a full recovery, we could have concluded that it was time to sit back and take it easy for the rest of our days. But Psalm 92:12–15 says, "The righteous shall flourish like a palm tree, he shall grow like a cedar in Lebanon. Those who are planted in the house of the Lord shall flourish in the courts of our God. They shall still bear fruit in old age; they shall be fresh and flourishing, to declare that the Lord is upright; He is my rock, and there is no unrighteous in Him." Whatever remains of our allotted time, by the grace and mercy of God, we will continue our journey and declare the eternal greatness of our Lord.

Whatever Remains of Our Allotted Time, by the Grace and Mercy of God, We Will Continue Our Journey and Declare the Eternal Greatness of Our Lord.

In all the situations and circumstances that I have shared in this book, as well as in all the others that I have not mentioned, it would have been easy and reasonable from a human perspective to look at a situation and think, "Woe is me for all the trouble I've seen." It would have been easy to listen to others say, "'The best laid plans of mice and men most often go astray,' so just stop, rest, and take care of yourself." At any place along the path to knowing more of Christ it would have been easy to stop and build self-focused monuments of self-pity to those things that had "happened" to us. We could have looked at all of the things that did not get done or all of the mistakes that I made or all of the things that did not get "corrected" and we could have said, "There is no use in going on." We could have stopped at any point along the way, but God would not let us. He continually called us to press on to know Him more and to walk in the fullness of His eternal and unconditional love, mercy, compassion, and faithfulness.

He continually called us to not let the discouragements, detours, or disillusionments of life distract us from the surpassing greatness of knowing Christ. He called us to not become comfortable or complacent in our relationship with Christ and thereby let the cares of this world cool the fire that once burned within us, but instead He called us to continually ask Him to fan the flames of love for Christ and press on to know Him more. For in the process of pressing on He showed us that discouragement means we had our faith in something or someone other than Christ; that detours mean we were going in our own direction rather than following God's sovereign plan and direction; that disillusionments mean we must have had an illusion of the truth rather than the truth of Christ; that complacency and focusing on the cares of this world mean we have taken our eyes off of Jesus.

Yes, in the Father's love, through Christ and by the Holy Spirit, we pressed on. But let me very briefly share a short summary of the major things that were necessary for us to do so.

Pressing On Required Focusing on Christ

It is a principle of life that if we are to finish something that we have been given to do, we must know the purpose of the task and everything we do must be done within the context of that purpose. As Christians, our purpose, our objective, our focus is Christ. He is Christianity. Hebrews tells us that He is the Supreme One and that as we run the race of life we must focus on Jesus, never turning aside until we ultimately see Him as He is. In Colossians 1:15–19, Paul shows us the Preeminent One as he says, "He is the image of the invisible God, the firstborn over *all* creation. For by Him *all* things were created that are in heaven and that are on earth, visible and invisible, whether thrones or dominions or principalities or powers. *All* things were created through Him and for Him. And He is before *all* things, and in Him *all* things consist. And He is the head of the body, the church, who is the beginning, the firstborn from the dead, that in *all* things He may have the preeminence." In Him "are hidden *all* the treasures of wisdom and knowledge" (Col. 2:3). "For in Him dwells *all* the fullness of the Godhead bodily" (Col. 2:9).

Christ had preeminence in everything in Paul's life; Christ was the focus of Paul's life as he gave all and did all for Christ. In Philippians 3:8, Paul tells us that, "Yet indeed I also count all things loss for the excellence of the knowledge of Christ Jesus my Lord, for whom I have suffered the loss of all things, and count them as rubbish, that I may gain Christ." Paul considered all things as nothing in comparison to the surpassing greatness (the excellence) of knowing Christ and he eagerly tossed all things aside that he might gain Christ. Even after all that he had done, he said, "Not that I have already attained, or am already perfected; but I press on, that I may lay hold of that for which Christ Jesus has also laid hold of me" (Phil. 3:12). Like Paul, in our journey Christ is the purpose of our life, He is the source of our life, and He must be the focus of all that we are and do.

Pressing On Required a Love of Scripture

Once again, words are not adequate to describe my love for the Holy Scriptures and thus for Christ. Scripture is where Christ is revealed to us from beginning to end as the only way to God, our only life in God, and our only truth in God. It shows us Christ as God perfectly revealed to us and it is in Him that we see the Father. It is where the Holy Spirit is revealed as God's empowering presence with us and without whom we have no ability to see or hear or understand Christ. His revealed Word is the light that we must have to follow Christ. It is the nourishment we must have to continue on our journey. It is the source of the true wisdom and knowledge to be found only in Christ. It is the revelation of our salvation, our sanctification, our healing, and our deliverance from the kingdom of darkness into His Kingdom of light. It provides the foundation of our faith, the guidance for our prayers, and the reason for our worship. It is our delight and our joy that makes our hearts burn within us as the Holy Spirit makes the truth of God come alive to us (see Luke. 24:13–32). His Word must be our constant companion to keep us on the path of walking with Him. As Spurgeon so richly says it, "The prayerful study of the Word is not only a means of instruction, but an act of devotion wherein the transforming power of grace is often exercised, changing us into the image of Him of whom the Word is a mirror."[1]

Pressing On Required Continuous Prayer

Everything that I have shared in this book includes many references to prayer. This should not seem unusual, but unfortunately many view prayer as important only in a crisis situation and rarely practice prayer as a part of their daily lives. What we have come to understand is that a continuous attitude of prayer is an absolute necessity in maintaining our relationship with Christ, out of which everything we do must come. In other words, prayer must be an integral part of everything we do. Prayer includes not just requests for immediate needs, but also, as we grow in our relationship with Christ, is a humble offering filled with praise, thanksgiving, adoration, and love for the Lord. In fact, as we come to know Christ more, our prayers will come to be less about ourselves and instead take more the form of adoration (acknowledgment of who God is), humiliation (acknowledgment of who we are before God), and then supplication for others (acknowledgment of what God has called us to be).

Christ said that He did nothing of His own initiative, but only did what He saw the Father do and only said what He heard the Father say. He was one with the Father, and His whole life on earth was guided by His loving, obedient focus on the Father. That oneness and its resultant focus were maintained and enlivened by His continuous prayer communion with the Father. And thus must our prayer life be in our relationship with our Lord and Savior. Following the example of Jesus, Paul and the other apostles, and those who have gone before us, we must pray without ceasing as we focus in loving obedience on the One who gives us life. Prayer is neither a vocal or a mental exercise for our benefit, nor a performance to show others how spiritual we are. Prayer is communication with the sovereign God of the whole universe as we submit our will to His and seek His will in all that we do.

As we press on to know Him more, we come to realize that a life without prayer is an existence that is cut off from the river of life that comes only from Christ. Since our relationship with Him and our abiding in Him are established, maintained, and grow through our continual two-way communication with Him in prayer, a life without prayer results in a life that is dry and barren and little more than mere existence. But a life filled with prayer is a life filled with His love, peace, joy, mercy, compassion, and the empowering presence of the Holy Spirit as we "continue earnestly in prayer..." (Col. 4:2)

Pressing On Required God-Given Faith

When Jesus raised Lazarus from the dead, Scripture tells us that He groaned within Himself (He prayed), lifted His eyes to the Father (He focused on His source), and in a loud voice called Lazarus from the grave (He moved in the power He received). (See John 11:1–44.)

As I lay in a hospital bed covered by a hypothermic blanket and in a drug-induced coma, the doctors told Joyce, "If he makes it, he will be revived in three days. But even if he does, he may have heart and/or brain damage." Faced with those possibilities, Joyce looked to her source and, being guided by the Holy Spirit power that she received, she prayed in accordance with God's will. She then held to the answer that she received until she saw the reality of it. This was not an exercise in vain, nebulous, human hope, nor was it some vague thought of what might be some time in the future if God decided to do something. As God had taught us through the years of His faithfulness to us, it was the exercise of assured faith that God is God. Though His provision was not completed nor seen at the time, it was assured because He had said it and it brought her His peace that surpasses our natural understanding. Then it was a heart filled with thankfulness for the word that He gave her to hold onto that would carry her through the opportunities to doubt God that she would be confronted with over the next several days. The faith that Joyce exercised throughout our ordeal was not based on her ability or what she could "work up" in herself. It was a faith that was given to her by God (see Eph. 2:8) and was therefore based in God and Him alone.

The Faith that Joyce Exercised Throughout Our Ordeal was a Faith that Was Given to Her by God and was Therefore Based in God and Him Alone.

Scripture tells us that "the just shall live by faith" (Rom. 1:17; Heb. 10:38) and that "without faith it is impossible to please Him" (Heb. 11:6). When we are in the midst of difficult situations, when our hopes for the future appear to have died, when we do not understand what is going on around us, we should not continue to focus on the circumstances but instead should come up to Christ and receive His gift of faith to go through the circumstances. Like the prophet Habakkuk, we go up to the source of all wisdom and understanding to *see what He will say* and how our thinking will be corrected (Hab. 2:1). We lift our eyes to Jesus, the author and finisher of our faith, the One through whom and for whom all things were created, the One into whose hands all authority in Heaven and earth has been given, the Lord of lords and King of kings, the final judge of all things said and done, the One who ever lives to intercede for us and who will never leave us nor forsake us. As we look to Him we not only hear what He says but we see what He says as He gives us faith to live by. Then, no matter the circumstances, we are able to sing Habakkuk's hymn of faith that he gave us in chapter 3, verses 17 through 19.

Then we truly believe with all of our heart and mind and spirit that we are to be anxious for nothing but in everything, by prayer and supplication, with thanksgiving, let our request be made known to God and that the peace of God that passes all understanding will guard our hearts and minds through Christ Jesus (see Phil. 4:6–7).

Then we truly believe that all things work together for good to those who love God, to those who are called according to His purpose and thereby walk in the fullness of God's lovingkindness (see Rom. 8:28).

Then we truly believe that our God is able to do exceedingly abundantly above all that we ask or think according to the Holy Spirit's working in us and thereby press on in that power that works in us (see Eph. 3:20).

Then we will respond to the voice of our sovereign Lord and press on to know Christ more and thus be more like Him and thus be about our Father's business as we walk by His faith and not by our sight.

Pressing On Required Waiting on God

I know it will seem strange to some that while talking about our always pressing on we would say that our pressing on required times of waiting on God. Like those who have gone before, there are times of waiting that are recovery from a difficult battle; there are times of waiting that are times of preparation; there are times of waiting that are simply times of fellowship with Christ; and there are times that are a combination of them all. Such was the period of years after we had, as I described earlier, experienced so much trauma in such a short period of time. But the trauma became the storm before the calm as we came into a time of resting in the Lord. It was a time when the Lord introduced us to W.A. Young Jr., Thd, PhD, and his wife, Ann, who by just being there for us and listening to us and giving us the wise counsel that we needed allowed us to rest and recover and regain our strength. Dr. Young also provided me with the opportunity for systematic study in which God opened the truth of Scripture and provided the foundation for future growth. This was not undertaken to be a church pastor but out of a desire to know Christ more. It was undertaken in obedience to God's calling me to the scriptural understanding that every Christian should have. The time of giving ourselves to study of the Scripture was a time of extraordinary growth in our relationship with Him and in our relationship with each other. It was a time when Joyce and I learned that revelation flowed out of our times of study and prayer in oneness with Christ and thus each other. It was a time of close fellowship with Him that drew us ever closer in our knowledge of Him and therefore in our love for Him. It was a time when the Lord renewed our strength and actually made us stronger than we were before (see Isa. 40:31).

Waiting on God is not a time of just standing still and doing nothing. Many of God's saints have experienced times in the desert or prison or isolation from others and found them to be times of learning and growth in their knowledge of God. Paul's time in prison was a time of waiting, but it was not wasted time as some would think. After all, they would say, "Paul could have been on the road actively doing what God had called him to do." But judging from the letters he wrote while he was in prison, while he obediently waited on God, he was actively doing what God had called him to do and it was part of his pressing on to know Christ.

We could have resented our times of waiting on God but He showed us that we are instead to see that such times are working for our good if we truly trust Him. In obedience to Him we waited for His direction and His understanding, actively doing what He gave us to do, resting in the knowledge that it is always better to arrive in the place that God has prepared in His timing than it is to arrive at the same place early and not be qualified to fulfill the Lord's purpose.

Pressing On Required an Attitude of Worship

Usually when we hear the word "worship" we think of a church service where we sing songs and perhaps are led in prayer. That is part of our worship and I love such times when a true worship leader takes us into the presence of the Lord. It is a place where our adoration of God goes beyond our natural ability to adequately express our love, gratitude, and reverence for Him. But true worship encompasses our whole life and is reflected in everything we think, say, and do. Worship is an attitude of sheer joy in doing all things as unto the Lord as we bow down in our hearts to the sovereign God of the whole universe, the One who created and sustains all things, the One who gives us each breath that we take and has brought us from spiritual death to eternal life. As we come to the place in our walk with Him that we see Him as the Supreme One, the Preeminent One, and see His "worthship," we then see that He is the only One who is worthy of our worship. We see Him as "the Lord sitting on a throne, high and lifted up, and the train of His robe filled the temple" (Isa. 6:1). We see Him as the One to whom "was given dominion and glory and a kingdom, that all peoples, nations, and languages should serve Him. His dominion is an everlasting dominion, which shall not pass away, and His kingdom the one which shall not be destroyed" (Dan. 7:14). As He allows us to see even a small portion of His majesty, His glory, and His splendor, our hearts cry out, "Worthy is the Lamb to receive honor and glory and praise," and we understand that He is the only One who is worthy of our worship. Then worship becomes an inner attitude of adoration, praise, esteem, honor, obedience, and reverence that flows out of our very being and out of everything that we think, everything that we say, and everything that we do. It becomes a way of life that gives Christ first place in everything and acknowledges that without Him we can do nothing. It becomes a whole-life mindset that focuses our faith, permeates our prayers, and fills our study of Scripture.

Pressing On Required Embracing the Extraordinary

Through the process of our continuing on this lifetime journey, as God has taught us that we must focus on Christ, that we must be guided by Scripture, that our life must be filled with prayer, that we must walk in the faith that He gives us, that we must wait on Him, and that our lives must be full of worship for Him only, He has also taught us that in all of these we were required to embrace the extraordinary—that is, going beyond what is usual, regular, or customary. He called us to respond to Him and rise above the usual, the regular, or the customary and embrace the extraordinary walk with God.

He Called Us to Respond to Him and Embrace the Extraordinary Walk with God.

It would have been normal to follow the tradition of lifestyle that I inherited from my earthly father , but God called me up to the extraordinary lifestyle received from my heavenly Father. It would have been comfortable for us to remain in the denominational church that we were part of for so long, but God called us up to embrace the extraordinary revelation of the Holy Spirit's working in our lives and His empowering us to truly see Christ. It would have been accepted practice to hold on to the pain of the past, but God called us up to the extraordinary deliverance of forgiveness, unconditional love, compassion, and mercy to be found in Him and Him alone. It would have been very common and acceptable to let the pressures of life destroy our marriage, but God called us up to His extraordinary nature of oneness and unity and sacrificial love. It would have been a normal reaction to look at the overwhelming evidence of physical injury or cardiac arrest and believe what we saw, but God called us up to His divine intervention that provided extraordinary peace in the midst of crisis, extraordinary faith for that which was not seen, and extraordinary joy in receiving His healing power.

The Bible is full of those who did not just accept or resign themselves to God's call in their lives but embraced His call and gave all that they were, all that they had, and all that they would ever be to follow Him. They cut across culture and even their religious cultural presuppositions to embrace their sovereign Lord and Savior and thus His working in their lives. That was His call to them and that is His call to all those whom He chose before the beginning of time to be His sons and daughters. He calls us all to see above the ordinary human perspective and live our extraordinary life in Him and Him alone. He calls us all to:

Rise up, O men [and women] of God!

Have done with lesser things. Give heart and mind and soul and strength

To serve the King of kings.[2]

Christ is above and before all things. All things are lesser things and we have been called to embrace the extraordinary and set aside all things to serve Him with all of our heart and mind and strength.

In our walk with the Lord, Joyce and I have come to understand that difficulties, obstacles, and crises and victories that He gives us are a part of life, but neither the difficulties nor the victories should determine the outcome of our journey. No matter what we encounter, God has called us to continue our walk with Him. Hebrews 11:5 tells us that Enoch walked with God and had the testimony that he pleased God. In our lifetime walk with God, we seek to please Him by our focus on Christ, our love of

His Word, our life of prayer, our faith in Him alone, our worship of Him alone, our obedience, and our embracing an extraordinary life in Him. Yes, we will encounter things that will try to distract us and that will try to entice us to stop before we complete the journey, but He calls us to learn from our experiences, our studies, our prayers, and our fellowship with Him and to press on to know Him more until we come to see Him as He is.

Final Comment

The experiences that I have shared throughout this book and the things that God said to us and revealed to us through those experiences are not intended to be detailed discussions of everything that God has brought us to. They are simple presentations of what I believe to be the primary truths that He taught us. Therefore, I pray that what I have said will be enlivened by the Holy Spirit to be a catalyst for further study and meditation by each of you who reads this book and thereby you may be as those in Berea when Paul and Silas went into the synagogue and preached Christ: "These were more fair-minded than those in Thessalonica, in that they received the word with all readiness [eagerness], and searched the Scriptures daily to find out whether these things were so" (Acts 17:11).

Benediction

Now to Him who is able to do exceedingly abundantly above all that we ask or think, according to the power that works in us, to Him be glory in the church by Christ Jesus to all generations, forever and ever. Amen

EPHESIANS 3:20–21

And my God shall supply all your need according to His riches in glory by Christ Jesus. Now to our God and Father be glory forever and ever. Amen

PHILIPPIANS 4:19–20

Now may the God of peace who brought up our Lord Jesus from the dead, that great Shepherd of the sheep, through the blood of the everlasting covenant, make you complete in every good work to do His will, working in you what is well pleasing in His sight, through Jesus Christ, to whom be glory forever and ever. Amen

HEBREWS 13:20–21

Endnotes
1. The Greatest Fight in the World, C.H. Spurgeon's, "Final Manifesto," p. 20.
2. "Rise Up, O Men of God," words by William P. Merrill, 1911.

About the Author

Steven Foster Graham is retired after having been a certified public accountant for more than 40 years. During this time he was employed by international public accounting firms and in industry, serving clients that included churches, ministries, and several large TV ministries. He holds a Bachelor's degree in Business Administration, a Master's degree in Biblical Studies, and a Doctorate of Theology.

As a layman, Steve has served in various positions in local churches. He has also been privileged to assist pastors and other ministers through teaching, praying for people, and exercising other gifts in congregations across the United States and in Kenya.

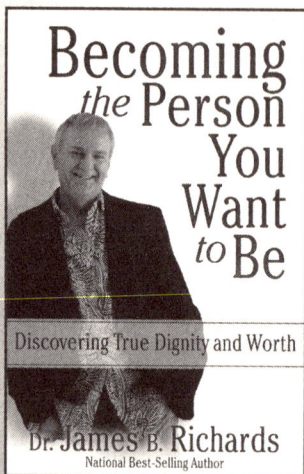

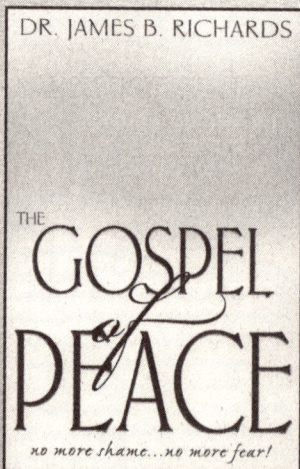

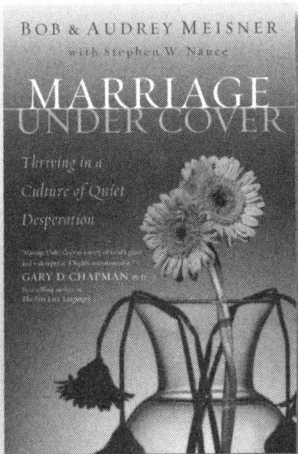

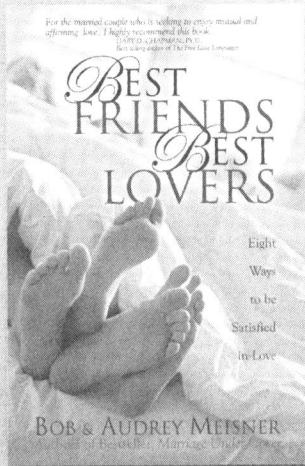